THE
FOLKLORE
OF PLANTS
Botanical Spells and Rituals

GREGORY LEE WHITE

White Willow Press
Nashville, TN

The Folklore of Plants – Botanical Spells and Rituals
by
Gregory Lee White

Text:
Gregory Lee White

Cover Art:
Gregory Lee White

Interior Illustrations:
various artists and illustrators from 1880s to the present

First Edition 2025

Published by
White Willow Press
211 Donelson Pike, Suite 111
Nashville, Tn 37214

Printed in the United States

ISBN: 978-1-965586-09-9

TABLE OF CONTENTS

OTHER BOOKS BY GREGORY LEE WHITE

Clucked – The Tale of Pickin Chicken

Making Soap from Scratch: How to Make Handmade Soap – A Beginners Guide and Beyond

Essential Oils and Aromatherapy - How to Use Essential Oils for Beauty, Health, and Spirituality

Little House Search – A Puzzle Book and Tour of the Works of Laura Ingalls Wilder

The Use of Magical Oils in Hoodoo, Prayer, and Spellwork

Papa Gee's Hoodoo Herbal - The Magic of Herbs, Roots, and Minerals in the Hoodoo Tradition

The Stranger in the Cup – How to Read Your Luck and Fate in the Tea Leaves by Gregory Lee White and Catherine Yronwode

How to Use Amulets, Charms, and Talismans in the Hoodoo and Conjure Tradition by Catherine Yronwode and Gregory Lee White

Lenormand Basics – How to Read Lenormand Cards for Beginners

Casting Love Spells – Rituals of Romance, Passion, and Attraction

Hex Appeal – How to Cast Dark Spells of Revenge, Cursing, and Damnation

Fairy Lore and Myths

Papa Gee's Book of Candle Magic

Cernunnos – The Lord of Wild Things

Hecate – The Goddess of Witchcraft

Tarot Magic - Spells, Spreads, and Sorcery Using the Tarot Deck

The Sacred Phallus – Magical Symbol of Power and Protection

INTRODUCTION

This is not a book about gardening. It's a book about power—living, growing, rooted power. The kind that comes from working with plants as spiritual allies, not decorations. The kind that demands respect, not romanticism.

Folk magic lives in the dirt. It's not always tidy. It doesn't wait for permission. And the plants that show up in this work don't care whether you're ready. They've already been doing their part—blooming at the wrong time, wilting when someone dies, showing up at your feet when you need an answer and don't know how to ask.

This is a guide for people who work with the land, the spirits, and the old ways—whether you call it conjure, rootwork, witchcraft, or something else that doesn't need naming. It's for those who understand that a rose is never just a rose, and that the wrong root can silence a curse or start one.

The plants in this book were chosen because they've been used over time—across cultures, generations, and magical traditions. You'll notice that some of them appear more than once. That's because, like people, plants have many sides. They do different jobs, speak in different ways, and follow different callings. One plant can serve many purposes depending on the path or practice.

So take a breath. Ground yourself. Read slowly.
!

DEDICATION

For all the witches who are good with plants—
the ones who know which leaf to pick, when to pick it,
and what kind of magic it holds.
And to all of you who don't yet know but want to learn -
This one's for you.

ACKNOWLEDGEMENTS

My respect and appreciation to the author, Richard
Folkard, who wrote *Plant Lore, Legends, and Lyrics* back in
1884. Your book inspired this book.

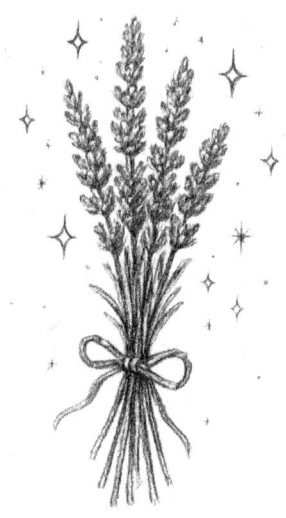

THE MAGIC OF TREES

Every tradition has a tree at the center of its world. You'll find it in myths, in prayers, in the way people used to build their altars—always with something growing, rooted, and rising. The sacred tree is more than a symbol. It's a map. A message. A reminder of what connects us to the heavens, the underworld, and everything in between.

In old Norse stories, it's called Yggdrasil—a giant ash tree that holds the nine realms of existence. Its roots sink into the land of the dead. Its branches stretch to the world of the gods. The Norns, those ancient beings who decide fate, sit beneath it and water its roots from a sacred well. That tree is alive, and it remembers.

In ancient Persia, they spoke of the Gaokerena, a radiant tree whose fruit gave eternal life. In the stories, it was guarded from evil and offered only to the worthy.

In the Bible, the Garden of Eden held two trees: the Tree of Life, and the Tree of the Knowledge of Good and Evil. One gave eternal life. The other gave wisdom—and consequences. Every magician should know that tension. It's the same line we walk in spellwork. You don't get one without being tested by the other.

In Hindu belief, the Ashvattha is a tree that grows upside down—its roots in the sky, its branches on earth. It's a way of saying: the world doesn't always work the way we think it should. Magic rarely does. If you're serious about walking this path, you'll need to learn how to see things from both ends.

These tree myths are more than just pretty stories. They are blueprints for how energy moves. Roots reach down, branches reach up, and the trunk—the center—is where we do the work.

THE TREE AS A MAGICAL TOOL

The sacred tree shows up again and again in magical practice, even if it's not named. Think about your altar. The candle is the trunk. The herbs or powders are the roots. Your spoken prayer rises like branches. It's a spell built like a tree.

Roots are about grounding. They represent your ancestors, your bloodline, the deep work you may not want to face. That's why so many strong protective herbs come from roots—like vetiver, burdock, or galangal. They pull energy down and hold it there.

In Appalachian folk practice, certain roots were dug with ritual and care—always with a spoon, never with iron, and never without first speaking to the plant. The root was seen as the "ancestor" part of the plant, and to take it without offering or acknowledgment was like stealing from an elder. It's still wise to leave a coin or pour out water when harvesting a root for magical work.

Branches are for vision and elevation. If you want insight, inspiration, or divine help, you need something that reaches upward. Think of airy plants like lavender, frankincense, or mugwort. They don't cling to the ground—they carry your words into the spirit world. In hoodoo, branches are sometimes used to sweep away spiritual debris or to strike out crossed conditions. A fresh dogwood or willow switch can clear stagnant energy in a way no broom ever could.

Fruit or seed is the result. It's what your spell produces. Every working should aim toward harvest. What are you asking for? That's the fruit.

THE TREE AS CROSSROADS

The tree also teaches us about crossroads—the place between places. In many traditions, that's where spirits dwell. It's where magic happens. The base of a tree is a meeting place. Roots and soil meet light and air. Life meets decay. Everything begins and ends in that in-between.

This is why so many magical spirits live in or around trees. You don't cut one down without permission. You don't ignore the tree that keeps showing up in your dreams. In hoodoo and other folk traditions, some trees are known to answer prayers. Others carry pain. Some help you draw love. Others can curse or confuse.

In the American South, folks used to nail jars, dolls, or coins into tree trunks as offerings or warnings. The "nail tree" or "wish tree" wasn't just a curiosity—it was a living altar. Sometimes a spell would be spoken into a hole in the bark and sealed shut with wax. Those old trees heard everything.

The tree responds to your intention. It's not good or bad. It's a tool. But like any powerful tool, it requires respect.

Ritual Practice: Root and Crown Centering

Before you do any spell that calls for balance—between logic and feeling, between this world and the next—try this:

1. Sit or stand still. Close your eyes.

2. Picture a tree inside your body.

3. From your tailbone, imagine roots growing down deep into the ground.

4. From the top of your head, picture branches stretching into the sky.

5. Hold both images at once. You are the tree. You connect heaven and earth.

Now speak your prayer or intention.

This practice centers you. It reminds you that you are not casting from ego. You are casting from connection.

In witchcraft, this may be called grounding and centering. In conjure, we might say you're "getting your spirit right." Either way, the principle is the same. You're aligning yourself with the natural order so the work you do comes from truth, not desperation.

These sacred trees have survived in stories for a reason. They are more than just tales; they offer lessons. The tree teaches us to grow, hold on, and let go. It shows us that true strength comes from being rooted while also reaching out. Be the tree. That's where the real magic is.

A ragdoll nailed to a tree. Often used as a warning sign

Offerings left at the base of a tree

TREES AS SACRED GUARDIANS

Some trees don't just grow. They guard. They stand like sentries at the edge of sacred places—gardens, temples, crossroads, cemeteries, and hidden groves. These are trees with a job to do. They don't exist just for shade or fruit. They protect. They hold power. And when you pass by them, something in your spirit knows it.

We see these trees in the oldest stories. At the center of the Garden of Eden were two trees—not one. One gave life. The other gave knowledge. And both were protected. When Adam and Eve were sent out of the garden, a flaming sword and a host of angels stood between them and the Tree of Life. Not because the tree was evil—but because it was too sacred to be reached without change.

In many cultures, trees are placed near altars or temples to keep the space pure. In old Hindu traditions, sacred fig trees were planted near shrines. In Celtic lands, oak trees marked holy groves. You didn't build near them without offering. You didn't touch them unless invited. And if you did, you'd better come clean.

In folk magic, we still honor this. Some trees won't work with you until you've asked properly. Others will open up right away—but the moment you twist their power for harm without reason, they'll turn on you. That's not superstition. That's experience. Sacred trees can bless or block. What they do depends on your intent.

In hoodoo and rootwork, trees like cedar, pine, and oak are often used for protection. Their bark, leaves, and wood can all be part of spellwork meant to guard your home, shield your body, or bless your front door. They don't just stand—they watch. And when you work with them, they'll teach you how to hold space the same way.

In Appalachian practice, the black walnut tree is known for keeping away what doesn't belong. Folks used to plant one near the front gate to stop unwanted spirits or guests. But you don't cut it down unless you're ready for your luck to leave with it. That kind of tree doesn't just root itself—it roots the energy of a place.

THE GARDEN AS A STATE OF BEING

In spiritual work, the garden isn't always a location— it's a state of being. It's clarity, peace, deep presence. And the trees that stand at the gate to that garden often show up when you're ready to step through. That might be the tree in your yard you keep dreaming about. It might be a crooked old cedar at the edge of a graveyard. It might even be a potted plant in your kitchen that stops blooming when your spirit is off.

In conjure work, cemetery trees serve as wardens. The ones near the entrance are especially important. Offerings left at their base can keep wandering spirits in check. Some rootworkers whisper names into the bark or press charms into the trunk to hold a boundary in place. When you enter that space, you ask permission—because those trees remember who came, what they wanted, and whether they were welcome.

In African tradition, the baobab tree is more than a plant. It's a spirit house. Ancestors dwell in its hollows. Offerings of milk, honey, or coins are left at its base. That same spirit shows up in the American South as the bottle tree—glass bottles strung along branches to catch evil spirits before they get inside. Blue was the preferred color, believed to confuse the spirits and hold them still in the light.

RITUAL PRACTICE – ASK THE GUARDIAN

Before working with any tree for spiritual purpose—whether in spellwork, healing, or prayer—you need to ask permission.

- Stand before the tree. If it feels safe, rest your hand against the bark. If not, hover it near and wait. You'll feel it
- a warmth, a calm, a soft "yes."
- Say who you are and what you need. Speak aloud if possible. Spirits, like people, respond

better when approached with respect.

- Leave something behind. A coin. A splash of water. A handful of cornmeal. A song or prayer whispered at the roots. Whatever you offer, mean it.
- Wait. Be still. If the answer is yes, you'll feel a shift. If the answer is no, take that answer seriously. Another time, or another tree, might open.

Sacred trees work differently. Some are generous. Some are strict. And a few serve as threshold keepers—you don't get through until you're ready.

TREES THAT GUARD THE THRESHOLD

These trees are known in stories and traditions around the world to hold sacred power. They show up near portals, crossroads, shrines, and burial grounds. And even today, their presence still carries weight.

- **Oak** – for strength, endurance, truth-speaking, and divine judgment. Oak trees are said to attract lightning because they hold power.
- **Yew** – for death, transformation, and contact with the underworld. Often found near cemeteries and old churchyards.
- **Ash** – for balance, fate, and travel between realms. In Norse myth, the World Tree

Yggdrasil was an ash.

- **Fig** – for wisdom, stillness, and inner awakening. In Buddhist tradition, the Bodhi tree—a type of fig—is where enlightenment happened.
- **Cedar** – for healing, purification, and contact with the Divine. Burned in rituals to cleanse and sanctify space.
- **Palm** – for peace, victory, and spiritual triumph. Often seen in sacred texts as a symbol of paradise or divine reward.

Every tree that guards a sacred space is holding something precious. A mystery. A memory. A mirror of who you are becoming. And when you approach these trees not just as plants, but as protectors, your practice deepens. You stop casting spells like they're transactions, and you start forming relationships.

So next time a tree gives you pause, don't just walk by. Listen. Ask. Offer.

Place your hand on the bark and feel the memory stored in its rings. Ask its branches what stories it's willing to share.

The trees that guard it don't just watch. They *test*. They will make sure you're ready to carry what waits on the other side. And if you're not—they'll keep you there until you are.

Buddha beneath a Bodhi tree

PLANTS THAT CARRY BLESSED POWER

Some plants aren't just useful—they're holy. They've been prayed over, carried into churches, laid at altars, and burned in sacred fires for longer than most of us can remember. These are plants that don't just grow in the ground. They grow in stories. In rituals. In the space between belief and practice.

When people talk about holy plants, they usually mean herbs and trees connected to divine power—used in blessings, cleansings, healings, and miracles. These aren't just folk tales. They're the tools of spiritual work. If you're called to the path of the conjure doctor, rootworker, or folk magician, you'll want to know these plants by heart.

In Christian tradition, palm branches were laid before Jesus as he entered Jerusalem. Today, those same branches are used on Palm Sunday, then burned and turned into ashes for Ash Wednesday. That's not just church custom—it's ritual fire magic. One plant, used in two sacred rites, carrying power through blessing and flame.

Hyssop shows up in Psalm 51: "Purge me with hyssop, and I shall be clean." It's used in both Jewish and Christian traditions to cleanse the spirit and remove sin. In hoodoo, we still use hyssop for spiritual baths, clearing away guilt, shame, and crossed conditions. It's a holy plant with a purpose—clean the inside so the outside can change.

Bay leaves have been burned as offerings since ancient Greece. In magic, we still write wishes or prayers on a bay leaf and pass it through flame. The crackle as it burns is your answer. If it burns clean and fast, your prayer is heard. If it curls or struggles, you've got more work to do.

Rosemary, once called the "herb of remembrance," was believed to grow only in homes where the woman ruled. It was laid on coffins, burned at weddings, and hung over doorways to keep evil out. When rosemary appears in spellwork, it's often asking: what do you want to hold onto—and what are you ready to let go?

These plants aren't holy just because someone said so. They're holy because they've been touched by prayer, fire, and faith—over and over again.

SACRED PLANTS IN MAGIC AND RITUAL

– Frankincense
People use this resin to send prayers to heaven. Its smoke rises, carrying words to the Divine when used in churches, temples, or rituals.

– Myrrh
This resin is often burned for healing, mourning, and sacred gifts. It is usually combined with frankincense to anoint the dead or bless the living.

– Cedar

You can use this wood in bundles or grind it into powder for floor washes. Its scent helps remove negative energy and brings a sense of peace.

– Rue

sometimes known as the herb of grace, rue is carried for protection and used in spiritual baths to remove the evil eye and break hexes.

– Basil

Draws love, prosperity, and favor. Made into water to attract luck and drive away envy.

– Blessed Thistle

Used to ward off sickness and sorrow. Strong medicine in the hands of the old-time root doctors.

– Agrimony

Turns back evil energy and breaks jinxes. When mixed with salt and thrown across a doorway, it can unbind harmful spirits.

Appalachian and folk traditions treat these plants like kin. You speak to them before harvesting. You pray over them before use. They're not just "ingredients"—they are allies. Living spirits that work alongside your will. They remember who gathers them and why. Treat them well, and they'll answer your call with power. But forget their spirit, and all you've got is leaves in a jar.

RITUAL PRACTICE – FIRE BLESSING WITH SACRED HERBS

– Choose three herbs known for blessing and cleansing
 Hyssop, rosemary, and cedar make a strong trio.

– Place a pinch of each herb in a fire-safe dish or censer
 This can be a small cauldron, cast iron skillet, or a ceramic bowl with sand or salt.

– Light a white candle and pass the herbs through its flame
 This blesses the plants with fire and sets the spell in motion.

– Speak aloud your purpose
 Say something clear and true, like: "With fire and spirit, I bless this space. With sacred plants, I call in peace."

– Let the herbs smolder
 Move through the space slowly. Let the smoke curl into corners, drift across doors, and settle around thresholds. Let the smoke reach every corner of each room and around each doorway in the house.

This kind of working is more than housecleaning—it's a way of putting your spirit back in alignment. A prayer in smoke. A spell that listens as much as it speaks.

SPIRITUAL RESPONSIBILITY AND SACRED USE

Holy plants ask for more than usage—they ask for relationship. You don't take them lightly. You don't burn hyssop just to feel pure unless you're ready to do the work of becoming pure. You don't light frankincense just to smell something pretty—you light it when you have something to say to the heavens.

These plants act as bridges between the seen and unseen. Between the dirt under your feet and the power that governs the stars. Every time you take them in your hands, you're holding a lineage—of prayer, of ritual, of wisdom passed down in whispers.

And that's what makes a plant sacred. Not just its name, not just its properties, but how it's been loved, honored, and worked with. How it listens when you speak. How it answers in fire and fragrance.

PSALMS USED IN HOUSE BLESSING

Psalm 23 – The Shepherd's Psalm

The Lord is my shepherd; I shall not want.
He maketh me to lie down in green pastures: he leadeth me beside
the still waters.
He restoreth my soul: he leadeth me in the paths of righteousness for
his name's sake.
Yea, though I walk through the valley of the shadow of death, I will
fear no evil: for thou art with me; thy rod and thy staff they comfort
me.
Thou preparest a table before me in the presence of mine enemies:
thou anointest my head with oil; my cup runneth over.
Surely goodness and mercy shall follow me all the days of my life:
and I will dwell in the house of the Lord forever.

This Psalm draws in peace, protection, and divine
guidance. It sets a spiritual tone of calm and security.
It's a favorite for home blessings because it speaks of
being led to safety and having all needs met.
Use it when: You're sanctifying a new home or want
to establish peace, prosperity, and spiritual safety in
your current one.

Psalm 91 – The Protection Psalm

He that dwelleth in the secret place of the most High shall abide
under the shadow of the Almighty.
I will say of the Lord, He is my refuge and my fortress: my God; in
him will I trust.
Surely he shall deliver thee from the snare of the fowler, and from
the noisome pestilence.
He shall cover thee with his feathers, and under his wings shalt thou

trust: his truth shall be thy shield and buckler.
Thou shalt not be afraid for the terror by night; nor for the arrow that flieth by day;
Nor for the pestilence that walketh in darkness; nor for the destruction that wasteth at noonday.
A thousand shall fall at thy side, and ten thousand at thy right hand; but it shall not come nigh thee.
Only with thine eyes shalt thou behold and see the reward of the wicked.
Because thou hast made the Lord, which is my refuge, even the most High, thy habitation;
There shall no evil befall thee, neither shall any plague come nigh thy dwelling.
For he shall give his angels charge over thee, to keep thee in all thy ways.
They shall bear thee up in their hands, lest thou dash thy foot against a stone.
Thou shalt tread upon the lion and adder: the young lion and the dragon shalt thou trample under feet.
Because he hath set his love upon me, therefore will I deliver him: I will set him on high, because he hath known my name.
He shall call upon me, and I will answer him: I will be with him in trouble; I will deliver him, and honour him.
With long life will I satisfy him, and shew him my salvation.

Psalm 91 is armor for your home. It calls in divine guardianship, keeps danger at bay, and reinforces spiritual boundaries. Use it when: You need powerful protection, especially from spiritual attacks, illness, or fear at night.

Psalm 112 – For Prosperity and Household Blessings

Praise ye the Lord. Blessed is the man that feareth the Lord, that delighteth greatly in his commandments.

His seed shall be mighty upon earth: the generation of the upright shall be blessed.

Wealth and riches shall be in his house: and his righteousness endureth for ever.

Unto the upright there ariseth light in the darkness: he is gracious, and full of compassion, and righteous.

A good man sheweth favour, and lendeth: he will guide his affairs with discretion.

Surely he shall not be moved for ever: the righteous shall be in everlasting remembrance.

He shall not be afraid of evil tidings: his heart is fixed, trusting in the Lord.

His heart is established, he shall not be afraid, until he see his desire upon his enemies.

He hath dispersed, he hath given to the poor; his righteousness endureth for ever; his horn shall be exalted with honour.

The wicked shall see it, and be grieved; he shall gnash with his teeth, and melt away: the desire of the wicked shall perish.

This Psalm brings in material and spiritual abundance. It affirms the blessings of a righteous home and sets a tone of financial stability, light, and generosity. Use it when: You want to attract prosperity and secure blessings for your home and family.

PLANTS OF MOURNING & FLOWERS OF GRIEF

When a soul passes, the flowers come. They line the altar, hang on the door, rest in the casket, and follow the dead into the ground. They soften the sharpness of loss. They give beauty where words fall apart. But flowers at a funeral aren't just decoration. They're messengers. Carriers of grief, love, blessing, and farewell.

The act of placing flowers on graves goes back thousands of years. Ancient Greeks laid fresh blossoms at the tombs of the dead to honor their spirits. In Victorian times, whole arrangements were made to speak what mourners couldn't say aloud. Every petal had purpose. Every bloom held weight.

In magic, we know that grief is not something to fix or silence. It's something to carry. Something to bless. And funeral flowers help us do that. They mark a threshold. A crossing over. And when used with intention, they also carry healing—not just for the soul that's left, but for the ones still here.

– Lilies
Symbolize purity, rebirth, and peace. Their scent and shape are believed to guide the spirit gently home. Used in spiritual work to clear heavy energy and bless the journey of the soul.

– Chrysanthemums
Linked to mourning across Europe and Asia. Often reserved solely for funerals. Represent death, honor,

and the soul's endurance. Each petal a layer of a life lived—some visible, some hidden.

– Roses
Used in almost every kind of ceremony. Red for deep love and grief. White for reverence and innocence. Pink for remembrance. Even yellow— once seen as jealousy—becomes friendship in death.

– Marigolds
Central to Day of the Dead practices in Mexico. Their golden-orange petals guide the dead home. Used in ancestor altars and spirit work to connect with the past and protect the living.

– Forget-me-nots
Small, gentle, and easy to overlook—but their meaning is strong. True love, remembrance, and spiritual loyalty. You plant them when you want to keep someone close, even after they're gone.

Other flowers often used in mourning carry their own sacred meanings:

– **Hyacinth** – for sorrow and forgiveness
 – **Gladiolus** – for strength and integrity
 – **Iris** – for faith, wisdom, and transition
 – **Calla lily** – for rebirth and divine beauty
 – **Carnation** – for love that survives
 – **Poppy** – for rest, peace, and sacrifice
 – **Violet** – for modesty, humility, and mourning

Placing flowers at a grave or on an altar isn't just a gesture. It's an offering. The scent rises like prayer.

The color draws the eye and the spirit. And even as the petals wilt, they continue to speak.

Ritual Practice – Grief Work with Flowers

If you've lost someone and want to honor them spiritually, try this ritual.

- Choose one flower that reminds you of them
  It doesn't have to be traditional. It just has to feel true.
- Place the flower in water or lay it on your altar
  Set the space gently. Light a white candle.
- Speak their name
  Say what you miss. Say what you remember. Say what you never had the chance to say.
- Let the flower stay until it fades
  When it wilts, bury it in the ground or release it to running water. Let it return to the earth.

You're not trying to erase the grief. You're tending it. Making room for it. Letting it move. Because grief is love with nowhere to go—and flowers help it find a way.

Some magical workers dry funeral flowers and save the petals in jars. These are added to oils or powders, used in ancestor altars, or sewn into protective charms that bless the living while honoring the dead.

In hoodoo and folk practices, graveyard work is sacred business. And when flowers are left behind—

whether placed with care or grown wild—they become part of the work. A violet growing near a headstone isn't there by accident. A wild rose bush in the back of a cemetery often marks more than just a patch of earth. Those blooms become the voice of the land, the whisper of memory made visible.

If you're walking through a cemetery and see flowers growing untended—daisies, violets, even weeds in bloom—pay attention. Those are spirit signs. Volunteer plants. Nature's way of participating in the rite. They remind us that life still pulses through the ground, and that death is not the end of connection.

In folk magic, we say the dead don't leave. They walk beside us. They appear in dreams. They shape the wind. And when we offer flowers, we aren't just mourning—we're in communion. We're letting the spirit know they are still seen, still remembered, still beloved.

PLANTS IN THE CHRISTIAN MYSTERIES

Christian stories use plants as important symbols. They are not just part of the background; they play key roles as signs, messengers, and sacred tools in the themes of life, death, and resurrection. Some plants grow in gardens, while others are placed on altars or made into crowns.But they all carry deep meaning for anyone who walks the path of spiritual or magical work.

The olive tree shows up over and over again in scripture. It stands for peace, endurance, and the Holy Spirit. When a dove returned to Noah with an olive branch, it meant the storm was over. A sign that God had made peace with the world again. Today, olive oil is still used to anoint, to heal, and to bless. In magic, it carries the power of cleansing and consecration.

The fig tree has its own mystery. Jesus once cursed a fig tree for being barren, and it withered immediately. That story is about more than hunger. It's about expectation. When you claim to bear fruit but have none to give, you risk being exposed. Fig trees became symbols of truth and judgment. They ask: are you living what you preach?

The mustard seed is tiny, barely the size of a grain of sand. But Jesus said it held the whole kingdom of God inside it. That's spell logic right there—small actions with big consequences. Mustard seeds are still used in hoodoo to cause confusion or stir up energy. But in sacred work, they represent faith in motion. You plant it. You trust it. You let it rise.

Thorns appear all through the Passion story. The crown placed on Jesus' head wasn't just a symbol of cruelty—it was a curse disguised as mockery. But even that pain carried power. Thorns protect. Thorns wound. Thorns speak of sacrifice. In magic, thorned plants often guard a boundary or ward off unwanted energy. The lesson is simple: what cuts can also keep.

In many churches, palm branches are laid down on Palm Sunday, then burned and turned into ashes for Ash Wednesday. That's transformation. Fire turning praise into penance. The same plant holds both celebration and sorrow. In magical work, that's the kind of plant that holds a double current—both a blessing and a warning.

– Olive
Peace, endurance, and consecration. The oil is sacred and used in anointing and healing work.

– Fig
Truth, fruitfulness, and divine expectation. Used in workings for accountability, clarity, or to call truth to light.

– Mustard Seed
Faith, transformation, and disruption. Used for

breaking blockages or planting new intentions in small but potent ways.

– Palm
Victory, sacred movement, and transformation. Burned to bring divine presence into the home or used as wards near the door.

– Hyssop
Cleansing, repentance, and spiritual renewal. "Purge me with hyssop, and I shall be clean." Used in baths and blessings to remove sin and guilt.

– Thorns (from rose, hawthorn, or bramble)
Protection, boundary work, and sacrifice. Sewn into protective charms or used to guard sacred objects.

In Appalachian folk Christianity, many of these plants were treated with both fear and reverence. The "prayin' women" who gathered herbs would speak Psalms as they picked. Olive oil was often kept near the Bible, ready to be prayed over and used on a sick child's head. A sprig of cedar under the pillow warded off bad dreams. A bay leaf in the Bible was said to bring dreams of your future spouse.

Some rootworkers still use the herbs of the Bible as part of their magical practice. Not to replace scripture, but to work alongside it. In these practices, the plant becomes part of the prayer—an extension of spirit through leaf and stem.

RITUAL PRACTICE – ANOINTING WITH SACRED OILS

If you want to bless a person, space, or object using Christian plant magic, begin with this basic rite of consecration.

– Choose an oil connected to scripture
 Olive oil is traditional, but you can also use infused oils with hyssop, frankincense, or myrrh.

– Place the oil in a small bowl or vial
 Pray over it. Speak words of purpose, like: "May this oil carry blessing, protection, and peace."

– Use your finger to anoint
 Draw a cross on the object or person, speaking aloud what you want the oil to do—"for healing," "for safety," "for truth."

– End with gratitude
 Leave the oil on your altar, or bury the remnants near a holy place in your home.

Plants in Christian traditions have been with prophets, provided shelter for saints, and marked the paths of resurrection.

If you listen closely, you can still hear their significance—in the rustling of palm fronds, the scent of olive oil, and the sting of a thorn. They continue to grow where faith has been planted.

PLANTS OF THE LITTLE FOLK

There's an old Appalachian saying that goes, "If you hear something in the woods—no you didn't." It's a way of reminding folks not to answer every sound they hear. Not every voice in the forest is meant for you. And not every trail is meant to be followed. Some paths wind through more than just trees.

In magical folklore, the woods are alive—with more than just animals and wind. There are eyes in the moss. Whispers in the leaves. Spirits that watch from the shadows and wait at the edge of knowing. Some call them fairies. Others call them the Little Folk, the Good Neighbors, the Hidden Ones. Whatever name you use, one rule holds true: treat them with respect. Always.

These spirits don't like to be seen directly. They live where the light bends—at the edges of fields, at the corners of streams, in the twilight between worlds. And the plants tied to their presence grow the same way. They show up at the in-between places. Not quite wild, not quite tame. Not deep in the woods, but just far enough that you have to choose to notice them.

– Hawthorn
 Known across Ireland and Scotland as the fairy tree. Said to be guarded by the Good Folk. Cutting one down can bring illness, bad luck, or worse. Some towns even rerouted roads to avoid harming a single hawthorn tree. That's not just reverence. That's survival.

– Foxglove
Named for the gloves of foxes—or of fairies,
depending on the tale. In some stories, the bell-
shaped flowers were worn as gloves by tiny spirits.
In others, the blooms rang like warning bells when
spirits gathered. Used in cautious magic for sight and
spirit contact. Not to be taken lightly.

– Fern
Especially in the form of the mythical Fern Flower,
which only blooms on the summer solstice in Slavic
lore. Said to bring hidden knowledge, speak the
language of animals, or reveal buried treasure. A
symbol of initiation and passage into a deeper
magical state.

– Elder
A tree sacred to both fairies and spirits of the dead.
In many traditions, you ask permission before
harvesting even a twig. It's said that if you sleep
beneath an elder tree, you might wake to the
Otherworld—or not at all.

– Toadstools and mushrooms
Particularly when they grow in a circle. These "fairy
rings" are said to be portals, dancing grounds, or
traps. Step into one uninvited, and you might be
pulled into a realm where time passes differently—
or not at all.

These plants and fungi aren't just scenery in old
stories. They're part of the spiritual ecosystem. They
show up when the veil is thin. When you feel watched
and can't explain why. When the wind changes
suddenly and the birds go silent.

In folk magic, you never harvest from these plants without asking. You speak out loud. You leave a coin, a ribbon, a bit of bread. Something in exchange. And if you're told no, you walk away.

RITUAL PRACTICE – MAKING A FAIRY OFFERING

To build a relationship with the spirits of place, or the Good Neighbors themselves, create a respectful offering space at the edge of your garden, woods, or any liminal area.

- Choose a natural spot
  Look for a place that feels quiet, still, or somehow different—where the wild leans in.
- Leave a small gift
  A bit of milk. A shiny coin. A sweet treat wrapped in leaves. A flower tied with thread. Keep it simple, natural, and sincere.
- Say aloud your intention
  Something like, "To those who walk unseen, I honor your presence. I leave this in peace and respect."
- Step back and let it be

Don't hover. Don't demand. Let the offering speak for itself. If you receive dreams, sudden flashes of color, or see animals acting strangely around the site, take it as a sign the offering was noticed. Not all contact will come in words. Sometimes it's a feeling in the wind. Sometimes it's silence lifting.

In Appalachian folk tales, the Little Folk aren't always kind—but they're not cruel without reason. They are proud. Protective. Easily offended and slow to forgive. But they reward those who act with care, who keep their word, who honor the old ways.

Plants associated with these spirits often have a dual nature. Beauty with danger. Healing with poison. Mystery with truth. That's how you know they belong to the Otherworld—they can't be pinned down. They teach caution, respect, and wonder.

And that's the real magic of fairy plants. They remind you that the world is larger than it seems. That not all power comes from the obvious. And that sometimes, the most important thing you can do—is listen.

THE LANGUAGE OF LEAVES

Plants speak. Not in the way people do, but in patterns, in timing, in signs. They show themselves in dreams. They lean toward certain windows. They bloom out of season when someone you love is about to pass. And the old folks noticed. They watched. They named what they saw. That's how the language of leaves began.

Long before we had books to catalog meanings, we had sayings. Wisdom tucked into phrases passed down through generations. These old sayings weren't just poetry—they were warnings, blessings, predictions, and prayers.

– "A green Christmas makes a fat graveyard." Said when the winter's too warm. If nature forgets how to rest, sickness lingers.

– "When elder blooms, summer looms." The elder tree tells time by the spirits, not the clock. Its flowers signal a change not just in season but in spiritual temperature.

– "Oak before ash, we're in for a splash. Ash before oak, we're in for a soak."

– A rhyme to predict weather based on which tree leafs first. A reminder that even trees can forecast rain.

– "Red sky at night, sailor's delight. Red sky at morning, sailor take warning."

Not about plants, but included in many farmer's almanacs alongside plant lore—because sky and soil speak to each other.

In Appalachian and folk magic traditions, plant sayings doubled as spells in disguise.

– "Touch a four-leaf clover and think of love, and your sweetheart will think of you."

A simple charm. But for those who knew the work, it was also a way of sending your spirit to someone else, lightly.

– "A rose petal under your pillow will show you who you're to marry." A piece of dreamwork rooted in divination. Especially strong if done the night of a full moon, or after a cleansing bath.

– "Tie a knot in grass to bind a secret." Said when someone wanted to keep their words from being twisted. Grass knotted near a fire could protect confessions.

– "Carry basil for love, but keep rue for protection."

Two plants, one to draw in and one to guard. A simple way to teach magical balance.

These sayings were never meant to be taken lightly. They were spells in plain clothes. You spoke them as you worked, and the plants listened.

RITUAL PRACTICE – MAKING A LEAF CHARM FOR GUIDANCE

You don't need a field guide to read the language of leaves. You need stillness, observation, and willingness to listen. Try this:

– Go outside on a day when the wind is moving but not harsh. Liminal weather is best—where change is in the air.

– Find a leaf that catches your attention. It might not be the biggest or the brightest. Let your spirit choose, not your eyes.

– Hold the leaf to your chest. Close your eyes. Ask a question. Don't force the answer.

– Watch what happens next. If the wind pulls it from your hand, that's a "let go." If it clings, that's a "hold fast." If it trembles but doesn't move, the answer is "not yet."

– Press the leaf in a book or wear it in a pouch Keep it until your answer comes true, or until it crumbles.

That's how plant language works. It's subtle. It doesn't shout. But it never lies.

THE PROVERBS OF THE GREEN WORLD

Over time, folk sayings became a way of remembering how nature moves—and how we should move with it. Here are a few more that carry deep roots:

— "Plant garlic on the shortest day, and it will chase away trouble all year." Garlic planted on the winter solstice is said to grow with extra power. A talisman in the soil.

— "If rosemary grows by your front door, the woman rules the house."

 An old English belief, still whispered today. Rosemary keeps order and memory. Its placement speaks volumes.

— "If the lilac blooms after a funeral, the soul is at peace." In some traditions, the lilac is a mourner's flower. If it blooms late, it's a message of rest.

— "Mint where it shouldn't be means trouble coming fast."

 Mint is invasive, fast-spreading, hard to control. Where it grows wild, something is about to shift.

In hoodoo and conjure, the phrase is often "the plant will tell you what it's for." And that's true. But sometimes, it tells you with a rhyme. With a dream. With a leaf that lands at your feet in the exact moment you're about to say yes to something you shouldn't.

BANEFUL ROOTS & MIDNIGHT BLOOMS

Not all plants are kind. Some sting. Some poison. Some whisper in the dark when no one else is listening. These are the baneful ones—the roots and blooms tied to shadow work, curse-breaking, protection through fear, and yes, sometimes cursing itself. But just because something is dangerous doesn't mean it's evil. And just because something is feared doesn't mean it's not powerful.

Every folk tradition has plants that belong to the night. Plants that draw out sickness. Plants that return harm to its sender. Plants that stir up spirits better left undisturbed. These are not herbs for the beginner. They demand caution, clarity, and deep respect. But in the hands of a skilled worker, they are some of the strongest allies in the garden.

In older magical texts, these plants were called "baneful," meaning they could harm or serve as warning. But the truth is more nuanced. Many of these herbs walk the line between medicine and poison. It all depends on how they're used—and who's using them.

– **Belladonna** (Deadly Nightshade)
 Glossy black berries and star-dark flowers. In large amounts, toxic. In tiny doses, once used as a sedative. Witches used it not to fly, but to shift consciousness. It opened doors—and like all doors, those swung both ways. Treat with utmost caution.

– Mandrake

A root that sometimes grows in human shape.
Folklore says it screams when pulled from the earth.
The scream doesn't kill—but the energy it carries
sure can shake you. Mandrake was used in love
magic, fertility work, and protection. If you can't get
true mandrake, ginseng or mayapple may serve as
symbolic stand-ins.

– Datura

A moon flower, blooming at night. Used in trance
work and dream walking. Its scent can lull the
senses, but too much will cloud the mind or shut it
down completely. Used in spirit travel, not sleep.
Only work with it if you know how to come back.

– Hemlock

Not just the plant that killed Socrates. In magic,
hemlock is used to silence gossip, sever ties, or end
harmful connections. You're not drinking it—you're
working with its energy through symbolic spellwork.
Hemlock cuts where gentler herbs only bruise.

– Henbane

Carries the weight of the grave. Used in death rites,
spirit summoning, and ancestral work. Some old
paths planted it by cemeteries to keep the dead in
their place. Others used it to walk among spirits
unharmed.

– Aconite (Wolfsbane)

Poisonous and protective. Said to repel
shapeshifters and evil spirits. Used in European folk
magic to bind harmful forces. A herb for the shield,
not the sword.

RITUAL PRACTICE – WORKING THE SHADOW ROOT

If you need to work with one of these plants for curse-breaking, defense, or personal shadow work, consider this symbolic method for safer handling.

– Choose a representation of the plant. A drawing, photo, or charged substitute like a black candle dressed in castor oil.

– Set the intention clearly. Speak aloud your purpose. "I call on this spirit not to harm, but to shield and reveal."

– Light a single candle beside the image. Let the flame stand as your anchor. If fear rises, focus on the light.

– Offer something bitter
 A sprinkle of vinegar. A black stone. A pinch of salt. Baneful spirits respond to offerings that carry weight.

– When the work is done, dismiss respectfully. Blow out the candle. Thank the plant by name. Cover or bury the representation if the work is complete.

Working with baneful plants requires you to understand your own shadow. These roots know what it means to hide, to defend, to strike only when needed. If you come to them in arrogance or desperation, they'll ignore you—or worse, they'll turn on you. But if you come with steady hands and a clear spirit, they'll show you how to survive what softer herbs cannot.

In hoodoo, some of these plants are kept separate from the rest. Stored in black jars. Marked and watched. Not because they're evil—but because their power is raw. You don't stir that pot unless you know how to handle the steam.

SYMBOLIC WORK FOR THE CAUTIOUS

If you're not ready to work with the physical plant, you can still draw on its energy in symbolic ways.

– Use a black candle as a stand-in. Dress it with oil and carve the name of the plant.

– Draw the plant on paper. Breathe on it. Charge it with your purpose.

– Speak its name in a quiet place. And listen for what it says back.

Baneful magic isn't just about causing pain. Sometimes it's about breaking chains. Sometimes it's about protecting what matters. Sometimes it's about facing the parts of yourself that others told you were too much, too wild, too dangerous.

But danger isn't always the enemy. Sometimes it's the teacher. And in the midnight garden, these roots grow tall.

PLANTS THAT DREAM – HERBS FOR SLEEP, VISIONS, AND SPIRIT TRAVEL

Some plants are rooted in the earth but reach into the dream world. They don't just calm the body. They open the gates of vision. These are the herbs of sleep, of trance, of spiritual wandering. They loosen the hold of waking life and lead you across veils, into spaces where the ancestors wait, where spirit messages drift in like mist, where dreams become doorways.

In magical practice, these plants are treated with care. Not all sleep is rest. Not all visions are gentle. These herbs can soothe the mind—but they can also stir the unseen. Used right, they guide you. Used carelessly, they confuse.

– Mugwort
The queen of dream herbs. Used for centuries in European and Asian folk magic to stir prophetic dreams, aid lucid dreaming, and protect travelers in spirit. Burned as incense, brewed as tea, or placed in dream pillows. She doesn't guarantee peace—but she guarantees movement.

– Chamomile
Soothes the heart and body. Draws in peaceful sleep, especially when the spirit is restless or afraid. Used in bath rituals and bedtime teas. Helps soften the edge of harder herbs. A gentle gateway.

– Lavender

Calms the nervous system, eases nightmares, and opens the third eye. In hoodoo, it's used not just for sleep, but to sweeten the energy around dreamwork. A pillow stuffed with lavender and rose petals is said to attract visions of love.

– Blue Lotus

Used by ancient Egyptians in rituals of ecstasy, divination, and sacred union. Brings about trance-like states, often with erotic or spiritual imagery. Some people steep it in wines. A flower of high vibration and deep mystery.

– Hops

Known primarily for its role in beer, but magically linked to healing sleep and letting go. In old folk practice, hops were sewn into dream pillows to banish sorrow and prevent wandering spirits from disturbing the bed.

– Passionflower

Unwinds mental knots. Brings rest to an overworked brain. In spiritual terms, it cools the fire of overthinking and helps the soul step out of the body more gently.

– Valerian

A powerful sedative in the physical sense—but a tricky one in dreamwork. Its scent is strong, musky, and disliked by some spirits. Often used in spirit journeying, but always with clear intent. Valerian can either lull you into peaceful rest or stir up buried fears. Know your reason.

RITUAL PRACTICE – DREAM PILLOW FOR SPIRIT TRAVEL

Dream pillows are one of the oldest and simplest ways to work with dream herbs. Make your own using this method:

– Choose a small square of fabric, preferably natural cotton or linen. Colors like blue, purple, or white align best with dreamwork.

– Add equal parts of three herbs. Try mugwort, chamomile, and lavender for balanced energy. Add a piece of amethyst or clear quartz if desired.

– Sew or tie the pillow shut. While doing so, pray or speak your intention: "Let dreams speak, let spirit lead, let truth come gently in sleep."

– Place the pillow near your head or under your pillow. Do not place directly on the face or too close to sensitive skin, especially with strong herbs like mugwort or valerian.

Not all herbs will give you clear dreams. Some bring only sensation. Some stir the body while the spirit walks. That's why dream journals matter. Write what you see, even if it makes no sense. The spirit world speaks in symbols. You'll understand more in time.

SPIRIT TRAVEL AND THE SLEEPING BODY

Spirit travel is not always intentional. Sometimes the soul leaves the body on its own when we sleep. But when you *choose* to travel, these plants become your companions and compass.

– Before bed, cleanse your space with smoke or water. Use lavender, rosemary, or cedar to quiet the room.

– Anoint your forehead with oil infused with blue lotus or mugwort. Speak your destination aloud: "I walk in peace through the dream gate. Let what is true come forward."

– Lay down with a piece of moonstone or amethyst beside you. These stones help keep the line between spirit and body strong.

– Trust the process. If the body shakes or you hear a buzzing sound, you're not alone. These are signs of shift. Breathe. Stay calm. And remember to return.

In Appalachian lore, people spoke of "traveling dreams"—the kind where you saw something before it happened, or knew something you couldn't have known. These dreams were seen as gifts, warnings, or messages from the dead. Plants like wild lettuce or sassafras were sometimes steeped into teas to stir these dreams—but only by those who knew what they were asking for. These Granny women of the Appalachians functioned as the doctors of their communities. They knew the correct and safe dosages for plants others wouldn't dare to handle.

Remember that not all dreams are safe. And not every spirit you meet is kind. That's why we approach dream herbs like we approach crossroads—with awareness. With prayer. With the willingness to turn back if needed.

Because these are not just bedtime plants. They are bridges that help you cross from one magical existence into another. And every bridge deserves to be crossed with care.

DREAMING FOLKLORE

1. Morning Dreams Are True
A common belief in European folk traditions holds that dreams occurring in the early morning—just before waking—are more likely to come true. "Morning dreams carry the voice of prophecy," the saying goes.

2. Never Share a Dream Before Breakfast
In Appalachian and Southern folk beliefs, telling a dream before eating in the morning is said to make it come true—or worse, invite it to manifest in the waking world. Keep it to yourself until after the first bite.

3. Dreaming of Teeth Falling Out Means Death
One of the oldest superstitions, found in cultures from Mexico to Italy, says that dreaming of your teeth crumbling or falling out is a bad omen—often foretelling the death of someone close to you.

4. Dreams Are a Spirit Journey
In many Indigenous cultures, especially among North American tribes, dreams are considered spiritual journeys. Your soul leaves the body during sleep and walks in other realms, bringing back visions, warnings, and teachings.

5. If You Die in a Dream, You Don't Die in Real Life—But You Might Be Reborn
Some old-world dream lore suggests that dying in a dream doesn't mean physical death, but rather transformation. You may be about to shed an old identity, pass through a major life change, or experience symbolic rebirth.

6. Dreams of Water Signal Emotions
In hoodoo and Southern rootwork, water in dreams is read as emotion. Calm water is peace. Turbulent water means trouble's coming. If you're drowning, you're overwhelmed. If you float, you'll rise above the storm.

7. Pregnant Women Dream Prophecies
There's widespread folk belief across Africa, the American

South, and even ancient Greece that pregnant women are especially prophetic in dreams. Their spirit is "open," and they receive messages for the baby and the future.

8. You Can Receive a Dream from Someone Else
In African American conjure and Afro-Caribbean traditions, it's believed that spirits—or even living people—can visit you in dreams. They might be sending a warning, asking for help, or trying to influence your thoughts.

9. Bad Dreams Come from Sleeping on Your Back
Old European and Appalachian folk say that sleeping on your back invites nightmares and sleep paralysis. It leaves your chest "open" to malevolent spirits or the "Old Hag" who comes to ride you.

10. Hang a Dreamcatcher to Filter Night Spirits
From Ojibwe tradition and spread through Pan-Indigenous teaching, the dreamcatcher is hung above the bed to catch bad dreams and only allow good ones to flow down the feathers to the sleeper. It's become one of the most iconic dream-tending charms in modern folklore.

11. Eating Certain Foods Before Bed Can Cause Prophetic Dreams
In Appalachian and European traditions, eating symbolic or "spiritually hot" foods like onions, salt herring, or eggs before bed was believed to stir up vivid, prophetic dreams. Some girls would eat these foods specifically to dream of their future husband.

12. Dreaming of Snakes Means Enemies Are Near
In both African diasporic and Mediterranean folk beliefs, dreaming of snakes is considered a warning sign. It could mean betrayal is close, someone's speaking ill of you, or you're being spiritually attacked. But in some traditions, it can also signal hidden knowledge.

13. Write a Dream on Paper and Burn It to Forget
If a dream leaves a bad feeling or sticks too hard to your spirit, old magical advice says to write it down on paper, speak it

aloud once, and burn it—turning the smoke loose so the
memory doesn't haunt you.

14. Dreaming of the Dead Means They Have a Message
Many folk traditions—especially in the South, Mexico, and
Afro-Caribbean belief systems—say if a deceased loved one
visits in a dream, it's no random vision. They've come with a
purpose: a warning, a blessing, or a call to be remembered.

15. A Dream the Night Before Sunday Will Come True by Noon
In old English and Appalachian lore, dreams dreamed on a
Saturday night—leading into Sunday—were considered
especially powerful. If remembered clearly, they were believed
to manifest by the next midday.

THE WITCH'S GARDEN

Some plants grow in the soil. Others grow in stories. And when you walk through the garden of old folktales and fairytales, you'll see plants that never show up at the garden center—but they live in the imagination just the same. These are the herbs and flowers tied to witches, magic, curses, and cures. They're not just symbols. They're instructions, hidden in plain sight.

In the old stories, plants were the secret helpers. A girl might be lost in the woods, but if she knew which flower to pick or which root to chew, she'd make it out. A cursed prince might need a thorn bush burned under the full moon. A broken heart might be healed with a red rose plucked at just the right hour. These aren't just bedtime stories. They are magical texts wrapped in rhyme.

Think of the tale of Rapunzel. A pregnant woman craves the greens in the witch's garden—wild rampion or parsley, depending on the version. Her husband steals the plant, and the witch demands the child in return. The message is clear: some herbs are powerful. Stealing them without permission has a cost.

Or Sleeping Beauty, who pricks her finger on a spindle and falls into a death-like sleep. But in earlier versions, the curse comes from a thorn or a plant-related omen. The hedge of briars that grows around her castle is both a barrier and a symbol. Plants can protect. Plants can imprison.

Witches in storybooks don't just ride broomsticks. They gather herbs, stir pots, and speak charms. The garden is their power source—and in folk magic, it still is. Whether it's a plot behind your house, a few pots on your windowsill, or a handful of dried herbs in a jar, your garden is where the story begins.

PLANTS OF POWER AND MYSTERY

– Mandrake
Shaped like a human and said to scream when pulled from the earth. Used for power, fertility, and spirit conjure.

– Belladonna
Also called deadly nightshade. Known for causing visions or madness. Used in flying ointments by witches, with extreme caution.

– Foxglove
Said to grow where fairies dance. Can protect or poison depending on use.

– Elder
Sacred to the spirits. Cutting it without asking first was believed to bring misfortune.

– Rowan
A tree of protection. Used in charms to ward off evil and enchantment.

– Mugwort
For dreams, visions, and protection from harmful spirits.

These plants appear again and again in tales and traditions, not just for their physical properties, but because they act as markers. They are plants of initiation. They call the seeker forward. They ask questions without speaking: Are you ready to cross the threshold? Are you prepared for what the spell will cost?

In many parts of Appalachia and the South, the witch's garden was a mixture of beauty and danger. Calendula bloomed beside pokeweed. Mint crept under thorn apple. Red roses were planted not just for love—but for blood magic, for strength, for secrets sealed with petals.

Some magical workers use the shape of a garden to cast spells before a word is spoken. A spiral garden becomes a path for trance. A cross-shaped garden calls the four winds. A circle of protective herbs— basil, rosemary, rue—creates a living ward that never sleeps.

RITUAL PRACTICE – SPELL JAR FOR OLD STORY MAGIC

To tap into the energy of the witch's garden:

– Take a small jar or glass vial. Clear glass works best. Let the contents be visible.

– Add dried petals, herbs, or leaves from magical plants tied to folklore. Try rose, mugwort, rosemary, elder, or lavender.

– Drop in a pinch of dirt from your own yard or a place that feels enchanted to you. Even a spoonful of moss or stone grit will do.

– Write a short phrase or question on a slip of paper Something like "Guide me through the story" or "What am I meant to learn?"

– Seal the jar and place it on your altar or windowsill It becomes a tether to the old stories—and a vessel for your own.

Some witches dress their gardens like altars. Colored ribbons on the branches. Bells on tomato cages. Carved sigils on stones. Each element holds intention. Even weeds are respected—because what grows without planting often holds the oldest power.

And sometimes, the wildest plants are the ones that guard the deepest magic. Dandelions growing through cracks. Thistles standing alone on hillsides. Vines wrapping a dead tree like a shroud. These are the plants that don't ask for your help—they offer theirs, with conditions.

In spellcraft, story plants aren't just historical references. They are portals. They help you remember that magic didn't begin with books. It began in gardens. In woods. In whispered names and careful hands. And it still lives there, waiting for the next person to kneel in the dirt and listen.

THE DEVIL'S GARDEN

Every garden has its shadows. Behind the roses and rosemary, there's always a place where the plants grow twisted. Where the leaves sting, the berries burn, and the roots don't welcome strangers. This is the Devil's garden—the place where cursing herbs grow.

These are not herbs for love spells or blessings. They're not for gentle hands or casual work. They are for justice. For retaliation. For protection when every other line of defense has failed. They are the tools of reversal, domination, binding, and banishment. But they do not come without cost.

In folk magic, you learn quickly: the same plant that heals can also harm. What blesses one person may curse another, depending on how it's used. That's the nature of baneful herbs. They don't play favorites. They serve will, not wish. And they demand that you mean every word you say.

– Asafoetida
Called Devil's Dung for a reason. Used to drive off spirits, confuse enemies, and compel someone to leave you alone. Stinks to high heaven—and that's part of the power.

– Barberry Root
Also known as Holy Thorn. Lay it across the path of your enemy to weaken their influence. Used to break controlling energy and free yourself from someone's grip.

– Calamus Root
In hoodoo, this is the root of control. Used to bend another's will, gain dominance in a situation, or speak so that others must listen. Often added to court case or boss fix spells.

– Dog Grass Root
Also called couch grass. Used in breakup work or binding spells, especially when entanglement is involved. Can be sewn into a doll baby to hold or divide lovers.

– Honeysuckle
Sweet, but not innocent. Known for binding lovers. Used to deal with infidelity, tie someone to you emotionally, or snare the wandering heart.

– Knotweed
A name that gives it away. Used to bind and trap. Wrap it around a doll, tie it in knots, and bury it to stop someone's power.

– Licorice Root
For compelling and coercing. A root of dominance. Used when you need someone to follow your lead or obey your commands.

– Morning Glory
Beautiful but choking. Also called bindweed. Related to High John the Conqueror. In its shadow form, it binds and smothers free will. Used to cause entanglement or block progress.

– Mullein
Used in spirit raising, often ground and substituted

for graveyard dirt. Protective when hung, but powerful in dark workings. Known as the Candlewick Plant—burns with purpose.

– Mustard Seeds

Scatter them at your enemy's door to stir up confusion. Used to sew discord, especially in relationships or court battles. Black mustard is preferred for baneful work.

– Poppy Seeds

Traditionally tied to confusion, distraction, and legal manipulation. Used to sow chaos or cause a person to forget or misstep. Associated with sleep, death, and illusions.

The Devil's garden isn't just a metaphor. It's a state of magical readiness. A space where you no longer plead for peace—you command it. Where you no longer ask for change—you create it. But like all strong work, it demands responsibility.

RITUAL PRACTICE – CRAFTING A BANEFUL SACHET

For spellwork that calls on cursing herbs, try this method:

– Take a black cloth or square of old clothing. Something worn and discarded, preferably from the target if possible.

– Add a mix of baneful roots and seeds
Try licorice, poppy, mustard, and calamus together.

– Write the target's name on a slip of paper. Add it
to the sachet with a drop of vinegar or war water.

– Tie the sachet shut with black thread or twine. As
you tie, speak your intent: "What you've sown, you
now reap. What you've cast, now comes back."

– Bury the sachet at a crossroads, under a thorn
bush, or throw it into running water. This sends the
working out with force, letting the spirits carry it.

Morning Glory

These are not "just in case" spells. You don't cast them unless you're sure. Because once released, they move like fire—and fire does not apologize.

In old conjure and Appalachian practice, you were taught to wait before working baneful magic. Give it a week. Let your rage cool into clarity. If you still feel the same after time has passed, your spell will be sharper. More surgical. Less likely to backfire.

And always cleanse yourself after the work is done. These herbs don't cling, but they don't let go easily either. Hyssop, salt, and cedar are good choices for clearing the air and sealing your spirit.

SYMBOLIC BANEFUL WORK FOR THE CAUTIOUS

Not ready to use toxic herbs? In fact, I suggest you don't. But, you can still work with their energy symbolically:

– Draw the plant on black paper and burn the drawing while stating your curse aloud

– Use a black candle carved with the name of the herb and your target, dressed in a matching oil

– Bury a mirror face-down with the image of the herb to reflect the harm away from you and back to source

The Devil's garden doesn't ask you to be cruel. It asks you to be deliberate. It gives you tools for when gentler magic has failed. For when justice isn't coming fast enough. For when the peace you deserve must be protected by teeth and thorns.

If you choose to plant these roots, do so with full awareness. Because they grow fast. They grow strong. And once they bloom, they change everything.

Wait a Week

They said, "Don't light the fire tonight—
let anger sleep, let wrath take flight.
The sharpest blade is slow to draw,
its edge honed fine by mountain law."

Let seven suns rise, seven fall,
before you answer pain's first call.
Let rage ferment, become precise—
not chaos-born, but cold as ice.

For baneful work, once cast in haste,
will spoil your hands, your soul, your taste.
But if it's justice, not just spite,
you'll find your spell lands clean. And right.

THE SAINTS GARDEN

Some plants carry the touch of saints. They've been blessed on church altars. Grown near shrines. Laid at feet of statues and tied to candleholders in the back of roadside chapels. They aren't just sacred because of what they are—but because of who they've been connected to. These plants are part of living prayer.

In folk Catholicism, especially in Latin America and the American South, saints are treated like extended family. You light a candle to them. You ask them for help in the same way you might ask your grandmother, your uncle, or a friend with connections. And when they come through, you say thank you—with flowers, herbs, coins, and devotion.

Each saint has plants they favor. Herbs they work through. And in magical practice, those plants carry not only the saint's energy, but their intervention.

– Saint John the Baptist
Associated with St. John's Wort, a plant that blooms at midsummer. Said to drive away demons and dark thoughts. Used in protection charms and to bless children. In some traditions, bundles of it are thrown into midsummer fires as an offering.

– Saint Joseph
Linked to lilies and carpenter's herbs like comfrey and mullein. The lily symbolizes purity and faith. Mullein, called "Our Lady's Candle," is burned in honor of the Holy Family. Joseph is called on in family and home matters. You plant for stability.

– Saint Anthony
Known as the finder of lost things. Associated with sweet basil, often grown on his altars. Basil for clarity, for returning what's lost, and for calling back love that's gone astray. A strong saint for reconciliation work.

– Saint Martha
The dragon-tamer. She's tied to herbs of power and domination, like calamus root and bold bay leaf. Martha doesn't ask—she commands. She's often petitioned with hot peppers and spicy oils to handle difficult people or clear a path with fire.

– Saint Michael
Tied to burning herbs like frankincense, copal, and dragon's blood. The warrior archangel. His plants are sharp, cleansing, protective. Used in banishing work and spiritual battle. You don't ask Michael to bless your home—you ask him to guard it.

– Saint Expedite
A favorite in folk magic. Works fast, often honored with red flowers, pound cake, and seven pennies. Herbs like cinnamon and ginger are used when calling on him. Saint of immediate solutions.

These saints don't live in the pages of a book. They show up in candles, in dreams, in unexpected blessings. And their plants do the same.

MAKING A SAINT'S HERB BOWL

To work with a saint through herbs, create a small bowl offering. This is a devotional act—a way of holding space for their help.

– Choose a small ceramic or wooden bowl. Avoid plastic. Let it feel sacred.

– Add herbs and flowers associated with the saint you're calling on For Saint Michael, try bay leaf, frankincense, and rosemary. For Saint Anthony, basil and white rose petals. For Saint Martha, red pepper flakes and calamus.

– Tuck in a photo, medal, or small candle. You can write your petition on a slip of paper and fold it into the mix.

– Speak aloud your request and offer a prayer or Psalm For Michael, try Psalm 91. For Anthony, Psalm 23. For Martha, speak clearly and with authority.

– Refresh the bowl weekly, and dispose of the herbs respectfully when they've served their purpose. You can bury them, burn them, or release them to running water.

In rootwork and conjure, saints are treated as powerful allies—but you build a relationship with them like you would with any other spirit. You don't demand. You ask. You show gratitude. You speak to them out loud, especially when no one else is listening.

Herbs aren't just tools—they're part of that conversation. A white lily on the altar says, "I'm still trying." A bundle of basil says, "Please bring him back." A pinch of rue in the corner says, "This house is guarded."

Spiritual medicine lives in the pairing of the plant and the prayer.

And sometimes, the plants bless back. When a rose blooms suddenly on your saint's altar. When your basil thrives even though everything else is dying. When your frankincense smoke curls into the shape of a wing—pay attention. That's a message. That's spirit in motion.

THE LANGUAGE OF FLOWERS

Before text messages, before love letters, there were flowers. Not just bouquets, but coded messages made of petals and stems. In the Victorian era, people spoke entire conversations through flower arrangements. A red rose meant love. A yellow carnation meant rejection. A sprig of lavender might whisper, "I forgive you." A bouquet could end an affair, ask for marriage, or start a scandal—without a single word spoken aloud.

But this language of flowers goes back much farther than Victorian drawing rooms. In folk magic, flowers have always spoken. They don't just carry fragrance. They carry meaning. Spirit. Intention. They're the quiet spell hidden in a corsage, the prayer folded into a funeral wreath, the blessing tied in ribbon around a wedding bouquet.

In magical practice, flower language still matters. When you work with roses, you're not just holding a symbol of love—you're holding generations of belief in healing, sensuality, grief, and divine feminine power. When you use violets, you're working with the energy of humility, hidden strength, and secret beauty.

– **Red Rose**
Love, passion, courage. Used in spells to inflame desire or seal a bond of trust.

– **White Rose**
Purity, remembrance, and spiritual devotion. Often

laid at altars or graves to honor the dead or petition for peace.

– Yellow Rose
Friendship, betrayal, or caution. In some traditions, used to signal a warning in love spells that are moving too fast or turning sour.

– Pink Rose
Gentle affection, healing, and quiet joy. Added to spell jars to soothe grief or mend the heart.

– Lavender
Devotion, cleansing, psychic connection. Burned in dreamwork or placed under a pillow to attract sweet rest.

– Violet
Modesty, protection, prophecy. Worn to shield the heart and strengthen intuition.

– Marigold
Warmth, protection, calling the spirits. Central to ancestor work and altar offerings.

– Peony
Honor, wealth, beauty. Used in glamour spells and to attract admiration.

– Daffodil
New beginnings, joy, and self-worth. Often used in spring rituals or to lift heavy emotional energy.

– Lilac
First love, memories, bittersweet truths. A flower that appears in dream visitations and divination work.

In Appalachian love spells, a girl might pluck petals from a daisy while whispering, "He loves me, he loves me not." But that's more than a game. It's a form of natural divination, where the flower becomes the voice of fate.

In conjure practice, flowers can be used in honey jars, sewn into mojo bags, or burned over love letters to seal intention. Some workers press flower petals between pages of a Bible or prayer book, letting the spirit of the flower carry the words of scripture deeper.

RITUAL PRACTICE – FLOWER PETITION FOR QUIET DEVOTION

If you need to speak your truth in love, or call someone to you with honesty and care:

– Choose a flower that speaks your message. Try a violet for secret love, a rose for passion, or lavender for peace.

– Write your petition on a small slip of paper. Keep your wording clear and focused.

– Wrap the flower in the paper and tie it with red or white thread. Red for desire, white for clarity.

– Place it under your pillow or in a sacred space Let it rest there for three nights. On the fourth day, bury it near your front door or under a flowering plant.

This kind of quiet work allows your intention to bloom slowly. You're not forcing love—you're inviting it.

THE SILENT VOCABULARY OF FLOWERS

Floriography gave us hundreds of floral meanings, many of which overlap with folk and magical traditions:

– **Camellia** – longing and perfection
– **Gardenia** – deep secret love
– **Forget-me-not** – loyalty, remembrance
– **Narcissus** – vanity or self-love (depends on use)
– **Heather** – admiration and spiritual protection
– **Hyacinth** – apology or jealousy
– **Tulip** – declaration of love (especially red or purple)
– **Chrysanthemum** – truth, fidelity, mourning
– **Snapdragon** – deception or strength in adversity

You can use this language in spellcraft to sharpen your message. A bouquet becomes a ritual. A floral bath becomes a story. A pressed bloom between pages becomes a bookmark for a chapter you want to write—or rewrite.

Symbolic Practice – Flower Reading for Emotional Clarity

If you're unsure how you feel—or how someone else feels—try this:

– Pick or buy three different flowers, intuitively
 Don't overthink. Let your spirit guide you.

– Place them in a row in front of you
 Take a deep breath. Look at them. Which draws your eye? Which do you avoid?

– Read each as a symbol
 The one that draws you represents your desire. The one you avoid represents your fear. The one in the middle is the bridge between the two.

Write down your impressions. Use what you learn to shape your next move. The flowers won't lie, but they won't yell, either. They speak in subtle truths.

In magic, we often think about power in fire, in thorns, in roots. But flowers are power, too. Soft, fragrant, unfolding power. Power that invites instead of commands. That listens before it answers.

And when you work with them—not just for beauty, but for meaning—you step into the same current that has moved through weddings, funerals, love spells, and mourning altars for centuries.

FUNERARY FLOWERS

Some flowers don't bloom for the living. They bloom for the dead. Walk into any funeral home or cemetery and you'll see them—lilies, carnations, roses, chrysanthemums. They aren't just decorations. They are messengers. Silent prayers wrapped in color and scent. Every flower laid on a grave is a spell of memory. A way of saying: I remember. I honor. I still love.

Grief has always had a language of its own, and plants have spoken it for us. They soften sorrow. They offer peace when there are no words. In magical practice, flowers tied to death are not only symbols of mourning—they're tools for spirit work, ancestor connection, and emotional healing.

As I'm sure you've noticed, many of the plants and flowers are repeated throughout different sections of the book. That is because they have so many different meanings to different cultures and magical traditions. I've tried to select the plants that you might be the most familiar with and have access to for your magical practice.

– Lily
 Purity, passage, and peace. Often called the funeral flower. Used to bless the dead and cleanse the sorrow of the living.

– Rose
 Love that survives death. The red rose speaks of deep devotion; the white rose of eternal rest. Petals

are placed on graves, burned in remembrance rituals, or pressed into ancestor journals.

– Chrysanthemum
In many Asian cultures, this is the flower of death. Associated with mourning, truth, and longevity. In some traditions, they are never brought indoors because they carry the presence of the departed.

– Marigold
Used during Day of the Dead celebrations to guide spirits home. Bright orange and gold to light the way. Used in offerings, garlands, and altars to honor ancestors.

– Carnation
Strength, remembrance, and enduring grief. White carnations for purity, red for admiration, pink for a mother's love that continues beyond the veil.

These are not simply flowers to be admired—they are vessels. They hold memory. They hold sorrow. They hold hope.

In hoodoo and conjure, flowers from funerals or grave sites are sometimes dried and kept for spirit communication or added to jars for remembrance magic. But you must ask permission before taking anything from the dead. Flowers left on a grave belong to the one who passed and those who mourn. You never take unless you're called to, and you always leave an offering in return.

GRAVE FLOWER OFFERING FOR A DEPARTED LOVED ONE

To honor the dead using the plants of grief:

– Visit the grave or a place where the person's spirit feels near. This can be a cemetery, an altar, or even a photo.

– Choose one or more flowers tied to their memory. Try lily for peace, marigold for joy, or rose for love.

– Speak their name and a short message "May you rest in peace and power. May your memory be a blessing."

– Leave the flower, or burn a dried version as an offering. The smoke will carry your message. The petals will mark your care.

This kind of work isn't just about mourning. It's about connection. It says, "I still walk with you, even from here."

USING DRIED FUNERAL FLOWERS IN SPIRIT MAGIC

Dried flowers from a funeral can be used with care in spellwork, but only for sacred purposes:

– Place petals in an ancestor jar. With their photo, a written prayer, and herbs like rosemary or myrrh.

– Add a few crushed petals to a candle for dream visitation work. Ask them to come gently, with guidance or reassurance.

– Use in grief-release rituals. Soak the petals in warm water with salt and rose oil. Bathe your hands, then release the water to the earth.

Each petal is a memory. Each scent is a reminder. Each flower is a bridge.

Planting Memory – Grief Gardens and Bloom Altars. Sometimes the best way to grieve is to grow something.

A grief garden is a living altar. A place where your sorrow can root and turn toward healing. It might be a small flowerbed, a row of pots, or even one plant in a window.

– Choose flowers that meant something to the one you lost. Did they love lavender? Plant it. Did they smell like gardenia? Grow it.

– Mark the space with a stone, a plaque, or nothing at all. Let it be sacred without needing to be seen.

– Tend the garden as a devotion. Weed it. Water it. Talk to it. Let the grief have a rhythm.

When you plant something in their memory, you're saying the story isn't over. It's just grown new roots. Because death ends a life, not a relationship.

GATHERING & DRYING PLANTS FOR MAGIC

The moment you cut a plant is the moment a spell begins. It doesn't start with the candle. It doesn't start with the words. It starts when your hand touches the stem. When you bend down and say thank you. When you cut, not just for yourself, but for the work.

Harvesting herbs for magic is sacred. It's not just about collecting ingredients. It's about entering into relationship—with the plant, the land, the spirit of the work. That's why timing matters. That's why tools matter. That's why intention matters.

You don't just grab a handful of leaves and hope for the best. You harvest with clarity. You gather with purpose. You dry with care, so the plant's spirit stays intact.

WHEN TO HARVEST

There's no single right time for all herbs. But there are signs.

– Harvest in the morning after the dew dries but before the sun is high. This keeps the oils strong and the plant vibrant.

– Pick flowers just before they fully open. That's when their energy is building.

– Gather leaves before the plant flowers. That's when the flavor and power are most concentrated.

– Pull roots in the fall after the plant's energy has moved downward. When the leaves begin to yellow, the root is ripe with strength.

– Work by moon phase if you can. Waning moon for banishing herbs. Waxing moon for attraction. Full moon for all-purpose harvests.

You can also time by the day of the week or planetary rulership:

– **Monday** for lunar herbs—dreamwork, emotion, intuition
 – **Tuesday** for Mars herbs—courage, war, protection
 – **Wednesday** for Mercury herbs—communication, cleverness
 – **Thursday** for Jupiter herbs—growth, luck, prosperity
 – **Friday** for Venus herbs—love, pleasure, beauty
 – **Saturday** for Saturn herbs—banishing, binding, shadow work
 – **Sunday** for solar herbs—healing, clarity, confidence

It's not about perfection—it's about presence. If you're aligned in spirit, the plant will meet you halfway.

HARVEST TOOLS AND TECHNIQUE

You don't need anything fancy. But what you use should be set apart.

– A small knife or pair of scissors, cleaned and blessed
 – A basket or cloth bag—avoid plastic, which traps moisture
 – A jar of spring water or a coin as a thank-you offering
 – Your breath, your words, your touch—all part of the ritual

Speak aloud as you gather. Even if it's just, "Thank you. I gather you for healing. I gather you for peace." Your words matter. They bind you to the work.

And don't strip a plant bare. Never take more than one-third. Leave enough for the bees, the wind, the next person who might walk that path.

DRYING WITH INTENTION

Drying herbs isn't just about preservation—it's about transformation. It's how you ask the plant to hold its power for when you need it most.

– Bundle stems with twine and hang upside down in a dry, dark space. Light fades color and spirit. Air circulation is key.

– For petals or loose leaves, lay them flat on a clean screen or paper. Turn them daily. Speak over them. Let them dry slow and even.

– Avoid using the oven or microwave for magical herbs. That's fast but careless. It breaks the bond you've made.

The dried herb is still alive in spirit. Treat it with reverence.

STORING AND LABELING

Once your herbs are dry, you store them like you would sacred texts.

– Use glass jars with tight lids. Label with name, date, and harvest purpose (love, protection, grief).

– Keep away from sunlight, heat, or excess moisture. This keeps their color, scent, and power strong.

– Add a pinch of salt or a small crystal if you're preserving them for long-term spell use. This helps maintain energy.

– Revisit your herbs regularly. Shake the jar. Speak to them. Let them know they're not forgotten.

RITUAL PRACTICE – BLESSING THE HARVEST

When you've gathered and dried your herbs, take a moment to consecrate them.

– Lay out a cloth and place your herbs in the center

– Light a white candle and say aloud:

"You were gathered in respect.
Dried with care.
Kept for sacred purpose.

May your spirit remain strong,
and your power rise when called."

– Pass each jar or bundle through incense smoke.
Cedar, frankincense, or mugwort work well.

– Seal them with breath, prayer, or oil. Mark the jar
with your sigil if you use one.

A worker's herb shelf is a sacred archive. A record of
your seasons. A library of green knowledge. It's more
than storage. It's testimony.

The plants remember where they came from. And
now they carry your name with them.

The Witch's Harvest

By moon or sun, with blade in hand,
I wander through the greening land.
The garden hums with whispered lore—
Each leaf and bloom, a spell in store.

I gather thyme where dew still clings,
For courage tied with silver strings.
I cut the rue with steady grace,
To keep ill spirits from my place.

A sprig of sage, both green and gray,
To drive the darker thoughts away.
A pinch of mint, for dreams made sweet,
And basil laid beneath my feet.

I pluck the yarrow, stem and seed,
For binding hearts and healing need.
Lavender, to charm the mind—
A gentler love, a will aligned.

The bundles hang from beam and rafter,
Dripping scent and spell and laughter.
The leaves will crisp, the roots will dry,
Their spirits caught before they die.

I tie them tight with cord and rhyme,
A verse to trap the breath of time.
For every stem was cut with care,
And offered thanks through whispered prayer.

So when the cold months veil the land,
And life lies still beneath the sand,
I'll call upon this summer's store,
And wake the greenworld's soul once more.

For herbs are more than scent and shade—
They carry will, and work, and blade.

PLANTS OF THE CROSSROADS

There are moments when your life feels like it's pulled in two directions. You've come as far as you can on one path, and now you're standing at a place where something must be chosen. That's the crossroads. A place of decisions, of turning points, of bargains and revelations. And just like the crossroads itself, there are certain plants that live at those edges—plants that don't belong to any one space, but sit between them, holding power for those brave enough to step forward.

In folk magic, crossroads are where the veil thins. They're not just intersections of roads—they're intersections of fate. And the plants that grow there, or work best under those energies, help you navigate change, choose wisely, or send a message in both directions.

These herbs don't promise comfort. They promise clarity. They open roads or close them. They test the truth in your heart. They're tied to the magic of liminality—that sacred in-between where transformation takes root.

PLANTS OF THE CROSSROADS

– Dandelion
Grow wild along every roadside. The roots dig deep into the soil, and the seeds fly wherever the wind takes them. Dandelion is used in wish-making, spiritual travel, and spells to summon the truth. It's a guide to future steps.

– Chicory
Another road plant, growing in dry soil and hard places. Used to open locked doors—literally and figuratively. Its blue flower is a symbol of hope in the middle of difficulty. In old lore, carrying chicory made you invisible or allowed you to pass unseen through dangerous situations.

– Yarrow
Grows in borderlands, between pastures and paths. Used for divination, protection, and making choices of the heart. In old love rituals, it was used to determine the faithfulness of a partner. A plant of boundaries, helping you know when to hold and when to move on.

– Vervain
Sacred to both witches and saints. Used to anoint tools, bless spaces, and break hexes. Grows near roads, rivers, and ruins. Vervain clears the way when you're ready to start fresh—and sweeps away what's been left behind.

– Mullein
Sometimes called witch's candle. Tall and striking, it grows along old tracks and forgotten roads. Burned for spiritual illumination and protection during times of uncertainty. A light in dark places.

– Devil's Shoestring
A classic in hoodoo, used to trip up your enemies and keep your steps steady. Planted near thresholds or carried when walking into unknown situations. Not truly a single plant, but a name for a group of

vine-like roots used to bind or protect at spiritual crossroads.

– Blackthorn

Not native to every region, but powerful in the story-world of the crossroads. Thorns for defense. Fruit for transformation. Used in binding work, curses, and breaking spiritual contracts. Carries energy that's both protective and severe.

THE CROSSROADS RITUAL IN PRACTICE

If you find yourself facing a life choice and want to do spiritual work at a crossroads, this simple ritual can help you seek clarity and direction.

– Choose a true crossroads—where two roads meet and continue in all directions. Avoid dead ends or T-junctions. It must be a place of passage.

– Go just before dawn or at sunset. These are natural liminal times. Day turning into night, or night into day.

– Bring a bundle of dandelion leaves, chicory root, and vervain wrapped in black thread. This represents your question, your power, and your willingness to listen.

– Walk to the center of the crossroads, stand still, and speak your intention aloud. Say what you need to know. Say what you're willing to give or release to move forward.

– Bury the bundle at the center if it feels right, or toss it over your left shoulder and walk away without turning back. This seals the work.

SPELLWORK FOR ROAD OPENING

Sometimes, it's not about making a choice. It's about clearing the obstacles so you *can* choose. Here's a rootworker's method for road opening using plants of the crossroads.

– Boil a handful of dandelion root, lemongrass, and basil. Let the scent fill your space. These herbs shake loose stagnation.

– Pour the cooled water over your doorstep or threshold. As you pour, say aloud: "May all that blocks my way be swept aside. May my path be open, and my steps be clear."

– Dress a yellow or orange candle with Road Opener oil or a mix of sunflower and bergamot. Light the candle and sit with your journal. Write down every choice you're afraid to make.

– Burn the paper in the candle flame and scatter the ashes outside at a crossroads. Let the wind take your fear, and the spirits guide your will.

DIVINATION AT THE CROSSROADS

Plant magic can guide you, but sometimes, you need a sign. Not from a book. Not from a deck. From the land itself.

Start with a dandelion puff. Whisper your question into it. Then blow. If all the seeds scatter clean and lift into the air, the answer is yes. If most of them cling to the stem, it means wait—things aren't ready. If they scatter unevenly, clinging in strange clumps or drifting oddly, the answer is no—or more complicated than you think. Pay attention to the way the air moves. That's spirit speaking.

You can also work with yarrow. Pull three stalks or leaves, each one representing a different path or choice. Lay them in a triangle on the ground. Sit with them. Don't rush. The one that draws your eye first is the direction your spirit already leans toward. That's the pull you trust.

Another way is with vervain. Take a sprig to the crossroads and use it to sweep a small patch of dirt clear. Watch what patterns the motion or wind leaves behind. Straight lines point to direct paths. Circles tell you that something's repeating—a cycle you're caught in. And if you see a fork, it means there's no avoiding it. A real choice must be made.

Let the plants show you what you already know, but haven't been ready to hear. They speak softly. You just have to be still long enough to listen.

THRESHOLD HERBS FOR
HOME AND HEARTH

Not all crossroads are found on a map. Some show up at your front door. These herbs can be planted near doorways or placed under thresholds to hold spiritual ground during seasons of change.

- **Mullein** to protect you during transitions
- **Yarrow** to guard against harmful influences
- **Devil's Shoestring** to keep your enemies out
- **Basil** to draw in new blessings and opportunity
- **Salt** and **chicory root** mixed together to stop backtracking and bad habits

THE CROSSROADS AS MIRROR

When we stand at the crossroads, we often think we're choosing between two roads. But sometimes, the real work is about choosing *yourself*. Choosing the version of you that's ready to grow. The path that asks you to believe in your own worth.

That's why these plants are so sacred. They don't choose for you. They offer clarity. They steady your hand. They remind you that the journey forward is your spell—and every step you take is an act of magic.

You don't need to know everything. You don't need the whole map. You just need to listen to what the plants are telling you. And take the first step.

SEEDS & SORCERY

A seed is the smallest promise a plant can make. It holds all the future inside it—every leaf, every bloom, every thorn. And in magical work, that makes seeds one of the most powerful tools you can use. They aren't just ingredients. They're blueprints. They carry memory, momentum, and mystery. A seed doesn't just become something—it *knows* what it's going to be.

In folk magic, we use seeds to represent intention. To hold the energy of beginnings, and to send that energy into the world with direction. Seeds are patient, but they're not passive. Given the right push, they will break stone to reach the light. And when used in spells, they can do the same for you.

WHY SEEDS MATTER IN MAGIC

Seeds carry deep magic. They hold growth, potential, fertility, hidden knowledge, and the promise of transformation. In rootwork and folk magic, seeds aren't just symbols—they're charged with intent. You'll find them in love spells, prosperity jars, cursing rites, and even in workings for justice. A seed's power is coiled tight, like a snake curled in the dark. It doesn't move until it's ready. But when it does, the shift is real.

There are many ways to work with seeds. You can plant one under a waxing moon to start something new. You can bury it with a written petition to help your intention take root in the world. You can burn it in ritual to signal the release of that energy—breaking it open so the spirit can rise. Some workers even feed spelled seeds to birds, letting the wind and wings carry the message to spirit. It's quiet work, but potent. And in the right hands, that tiny shell becomes a living force.

SEEDS AND THEIR MAGICAL MEANINGS

– Mustard Seeds
For faith, confusion, or disruption. Used in both blessing and baneful work. Scatter them to create spiritual confusion or carry them to keep faith when the path is unclear.

– Poppy Seeds
For sleep, forgetfulness, and distraction. Used to create confusion in court cases or to cloud judgment. Also tied to death, dreams, and altered states of awareness.

– Pumpkin Seeds
For fertility, abundance, and protection. Can be planted in prosperity spells or carried for financial luck. Roast them and add them to spell powders for growth energy.

– Apple Seeds
For love, knowledge, and temptation. A single apple seed placed in a love charm can call a heart toward you. Also used in spells that seek truth.

– Coriander Seeds
Used in love and lust magic. Tied to long-term

relationships and strengthening commitment. Often sewn into sachets or carried in lockets.

– Caraway Seeds
For fidelity and protection. In traditional folk magic, placing caraway in a lover's food was believed to keep them faithful. Also useful in baby blessings and home protection work.

– Dill Seeds
Used for defense, clearing gossip, and drawing blessings. In Eastern European and Appalachian work, dill seeds were placed in shoes to walk away from slander.

– Sunflower Seeds
For hope, light, confidence, and attention. Great in work to boost self-esteem or to be noticed. They follow the sun, and in magic, help you stay aligned with your goal.

– Wheat Berries
Symbolize prosperity and spiritual nourishment. Used in rituals tied to harvest, gratitude, and sustenance. Often added to cornucopias or abundance altars.

SEED JAR FOR NEW BEGINNINGS

This is a simple working, but don't let that fool you. It's potent. It lets you plant the future you want— literally and symbolically. Start with a small glass jar and fill it halfway with fertile dirt. Choose a single seed that matches your goal. Pumpkin is good for prosperity. Poppy brings peace. Sunflower draws in confidence and boldness. Hold the seed in your hand and speak your intention out loud: "I plant this hope. I plant this truth. I plant the life I want to grow." Then bury the seed gently in the jar, close the lid, and place it somewhere it can catch sunlight. Give it just a few drops of water at a time. No flooding. Just enough to keep it alive.

Then wait. Watch. When the first green breaks through, that's your sign—the spell is taking root, the work is in motion. But if nothing grows, that's a message too. It might mean you're forcing what isn't ready. Or that something in you needs clearing first. Either way, planting is an act of faith. It's a sacred beginning. The dirt remembers. And the seed always knows when to rise.

SEED POUCH FOR STRENGTH AND STABILITY

Sometimes you need to carry a spell with you—not in fire or smoke, but in quiet weight. Seeds are perfect for that.

– Take a small square of cloth and place in it:
 – 3 sunflower seeds (for courage)
 – 7 caraway seeds (for protection)
 – A pinch of mustard seed (for spiritual clarity)
 – Add a personal concern—hair, handwriting, a drop of oil
 – Tie it shut and carry it on your person, especially during hard transitions

You can sleep with this pouch under your pillow when you're making big decisions. Replace the seeds each moon cycle for continued strength.

SEED BANISHMENT RITUAL

If there's something you need to be free from—a harmful habit, a toxic relationship, or a thought that keeps circling back like a curse—this working can help release it. Start by writing what you want to let go of on a slip of brown paper. Be specific. Fold that paper around a single poppy seed or mustard seed, something small but full of force. Then spit on the bundle. Yes, spit. Life fluid. It carries your will, your refusal, your break with what no longer serves. Bury the bundle at a crossroads, or under a stone where nothing grows. Let the earth take it. As the paper rots and the seed dissolves, the tie weakens. And then, with time, it breaks.

SACRED SEED LORE FROM TRADITION

In hoodoo, mustard seeds are traditionally used in confusion and war magic. These small but potent seeds are often sprinkled across doorways to sow discord, placed in sour jars to intensify bitterness, or added to "shut your mouth" workings to silence gossip and slander. Their disruptive energy makes them ideal for stirring mental unrest and blocking communication in someone's life.

Appalachian folk traditions hold pumpkin and corn seeds as symbols of prosperity, especially for those who till the land. Carried in pockets or tied into small charm bags, these seeds serve as a blessing for good harvests and financial growth. A pouch of cornmeal and seed is sometimes tied into the belt of someone launching a new business, offering not just hope but a tangible connection to the cycles of abundance.

In Mexican folk Catholicism, coriander and caraway seeds are tied into small pieces of cloth and placed on children's cribs as protection against the evil eye. This practice blends Catholic devotional symbols with ancient indigenous protections, showing the seamless fusion of spirituality and daily life. The aroma of these seeds, along with their magical associations, serves to shield the child from harm and spiritual intrusion.

In West African-rooted traditions, seeds carry sacred meaning tied to sacrifice, renewal, and ancestral offering. A handful of sesame, millet, or okra seed may be placed on ancestral altars to nourish and honor the spirits of those who came before. These seeds are not merely symbols of life—they are living offerings, connecting the physical and spiritual through acts of remembrance and reverence.

BLESSING THE SEEDS BEFORE USE

Just like herbs, seeds should be awakened before magical work.

– Hold the seed in your palm
 – Breathe on it slowly three times
 – Speak to it: "Wake up, little one. Grow for me."
 – Pass it through incense or water for cleansing
 – Then begin your work

This creates a bond. You're not just using a tool—you're calling on a partner.

HARVESTING AND SAVING YOUR OWN SEEDS

If you grow your own plants, save seeds for magic: Choose seeds from the strongest plants, the ones that bloomed brightest or bore the most fruit. Dry them completely on paper or cloth. Store in small glass jars, paper envelopes, or seed pouches. Label with the plant name, date, and purpose: "Basil – Grown for love – Full Moon Harvest." Each year, replant a few. This keeps the cycle going. Magic should never be still. It should grow.

RITUAL: SEEDS OF THE ANCESTORS

To honor your lineage and call on ancestral help, begin with a handful of seeds. Any kind will do, as long as they're whole and alive. Step into a quiet space—somewhere sacred, outside if you can—and speak the names of those who walked before you. As you scatter the seeds in a circle or within your chosen space, let each one fall with the words, "I remember." Say it out loud. Let it land. The birds, the wind, and the earth will carry those seeds, and with them, your message. You don't need to explain yourself. Your ancestors will know exactly what you're saying.

In Appalachian communities, neighbors would often gather in early spring or late harvest for seed swaps—bringing jars, envelopes, or hand-sewn pouches filled with heirloom seeds passed down through generations. These gatherings weren't just about planting; they were about preserving heritage, sharing knowledge, and ensuring everyone had what they needed for the coming season. Folks would also help one another dry, sort, and store seeds properly, often using paper, ash, or cloth to keep them safe from moisture and pests.

MAGICAL TREES OF THE AMERICAS

Some spirits stand taller than the rest. They don't bloom small. They tower. They watch. They root deep in the earth and reach high into the heavens. These are the trees—not just plants, but whole presences unto themselves. Where herbs whisper and vines climb, trees hold. They anchor. They carry stories in their bark and memory in their rings.

In American folk magic—from the hills of Appalachia to the jungles of Brazil—certain trees have earned a sacred place. They are protectors. Teachers. Portals. You don't walk past them without offering something. And if you're wise, you never cut their wood without asking permission. Because some trees will forgive you. Others will not.

The Black Walnut – The Warden of Secrets

Black walnut is no soft ally. Its shell is hard. Its branches loom. Its roots release a chemical that keeps other plants from growing too close. In folk tradition, walnut is used to separate, protect, and drive out. If you're looking to cut ties or banish something that won't let go, this is your tree. Carry a black walnut shell to break ties with a toxic lover. Write a name on a walnut leaf and bury it at a crossroads. Wash your hands in walnut bark tea to remove spiritual residue. The tree itself is a solitary spirit. It doesn't tolerate clinginess—neither in plants nor people. If you need a clean break, this is the tree to call.

The Ceiba – Tree of Spirits and Sky

In Afro-Caribbean and Central American lore, the ceiba (or kapok tree) is the axis mundi—the world tree. Its roots reach into the dead. Its crown touches the heavens. Spirits live in its trunk. In some traditions, you don't even point at it, lest you offend what's watching from within. Ceiba bark is used in spiritual baths for protection and ancestral connection. The cotton from its seed pods is sometimes used to dress dolls for spirit work. Sacred to many African Traditional Religions and Indigenous groups across the Americas, the ceiba is a tree you approach slowly, with reverence. Because it does not forget who walks beneath it.

Sassafras – The Road Opener

Sassafras smells like root beer and old wisdom. In Appalachian conjure, it's considered a road-opener plant. Its leaves, bark, and root are used in workings to bring luck, clear a path, or welcome new beginnings. Brew a tea from the bark (non-toxic varieties only) and use it in a floor wash for good luck. Carry a dried root in your pocket when starting a journey or new job. Burn sassafras chips as an offering to ancestors or spirits of the land. This is a friendly tree. A talkative one. It likes to help—but it still expects gratitude. Leave a coin, a song, or a breath of thanks when you take.

The Palo Santo – Holy Stick of the Andes

Palo santo comes from South America, particularly Ecuador and Peru. It's the wood of a tree in the citrus family, and its name means "holy wood." It's burned like incense to cleanse, protect, and call in blessings. Burn palo santo to lift heavy energy. Use its ash in protective powders or to dress candles. Combine with copal resin for ancestral communication. But this tree is sacred. You don't just break a branch. You only use the wood that falls naturally. Anything else carries trouble. In fact, most reputable suppliers will only harvest deadwood. The living tree isn't to be touched.

The Joshua Tree – Desert Guardian

Out west, in the Mojave and Sonoran deserts, the Joshua Tree stands like a sentinel. Strange, spiky, and otherworldly, it has long been tied to prophecy and spiritual testing. Sit beneath a Joshua Tree to receive visions or answers during fasts. Leave an offering at its base when doing desert magic or spirit walking. In folk legend, these trees are believed to mark paths of power or sacred sites. It doesn't grow where the spirit is weak. And it doesn't tolerate haste. This tree teaches you to slow down and listen.

The Dogwood – Tree of Sacrifice

In Southern folklore, the dogwood is tied to the crucifixion of Christ. Its petals form the shape of a cross, and the center bears the mark of a crown of thorns. It's a tree of sacrifice and spiritual healing. Use dogwood branches in rituals of forgiveness. Carve crosses from its twigs to protect the home. Burn its dried blossoms during Lenten prayers or Easter rituals. Some traditions say dogwood is cursed, others say it is blessed. But either way, it holds pain and grace in equal measure.

The Witch-Hazel – Healer and Seer

Witch-hazel is best known for its healing bark and divinatory uses. In both folk medicine and magic, it's used to soothe the skin and reveal hidden things. Use twigs as dowsing rods to find water or buried items. Make an infusion of bark and leaves for use in healing spells. Carry a bit in your pocket when seeking the truth or unraveling a lie. In magical terms, witch-hazel is a revealer. It won't curse, but it won't let you keep secrets either.

TREE MAGIC IN RITUAL AND PRACTICE

When you work with trees in spellcraft, you're not just using ingredients. You're forming a relationship. These spirits are older than you. Older than your grandmother's grandmother. They remember what you've forgotten.

To gather respectfully, always ask before cutting or taking bark, leaves, or wood. Leave an offering— coin, water, tobacco, or a strand of hair. Speak the name of the tree if you know it. Speak your name in return.

To make tree water, take a small piece of bark or a handful of leaves. Soak them in spring water under the moon overnight. Strain and use to cleanse tools, dress candles, or anoint your hands.

To create a bark bundle for protection, combine bark from oak (strength), black walnut (banishing), and sassafras (clearing). Tie together with red thread.

Hang near the front door or above your altar. This bundle becomes a living prayer. A ward that watches.

SPIRITUAL PRACTICES AT THE ROOTS

Tree roots don't just feed the plant—they reach into the otherworld. In the old ways of conjure, this truth isn't just poetic—it's practical. Roots are messengers. They carry intention, energy, and prayer down into the deep places, the places where spirits dwell and old power sleeps. That's why we bury things beneath trees—not just to hide them, but to send them. When you place a name paper under a tree, you're not just working with the tree. You're working with what's beneath it. You're asking the earth to hold your will and do something with it.

If you're trying to grow something—be it love, healing, money, or a sense of purpose—you bury that work under an oak or an apple tree. Oak stands strong. Apple blesses with sweetness. Their roots are friendly to fruitfulness. But if you're trying to end something—to shut a door, to sever a tie, to make something go away—you go to a black walnut, a cedar, or a pine. Black walnut doesn't suffer clingers. Cedar clears. Pine purifies. These are trees that know how to push things out.

And then there are the trees that listen to the dead. Sit at the base of a willow, and the grief of generations might rise up to meet you. Lean your back against a cypress, and you may hear something whisper back. Ceiba, in particular, stands as the world tree in many traditions—its roots in the underworld, its branches in the heavens. When you bury something there, it doesn't just go into the ground. It crosses a threshold.

When we bury under a tree, we're not just doing a trick. We're entering a pact—with earth, with spirit, with time itself. And what we plant doesn't just stay where we left it. It grows. Or it dissolves. Or it travels. Because roots don't just anchor. They move. They reach. And they remember.

A Joshua tree

WATERS & WEEDS – RIVERBANK MAGIC

Magic gathers at the edges. Where one thing becomes another—where land becomes water, where forest meets field, where dusk falls between the hours— these are the places where spirits stir. The riverbank is one of those thresholds. It's a place of motion, of memory, of mystery. The land doesn't end there. It lets go. And water carries what the earth can't hold anymore.

That's why so many spells are cast by water. That's why we bury our sorrow at the river's mouth, why we toss coins and whispers into the current, and why weeds that grow along the shore are often more powerful than any cultivated herb in a garden.

These plants drink from a different well. They grow with one foot in the seen and one in the unseen. You don't plant them—they volunteer. And anything that chooses to grow between the worlds is worth listening to.

THE MAGIC OF RIVER PLANTS

Here are a few common waterside plants that have long held power in folk magic:

– Willow
 A tree of grief, flexibility, and sacred binding. Its bark eases pain; its branches make excellent cords for knot magic. In many traditions, you whisper your sorrow into the trunk and let the river carry it away.

– Boneset

Used to break fevers and call healing spirits. The name itself suggests restoration. In magical work, it's used to mend what's been broken—not just bones, but trust, relationships, and hope.

– Cattail

Tall and sturdy, yet swaying with the wind. Symbolic of survival and quiet strength. A cattail's fuzz was once used as insulation, and in spellwork, it can be used to pad and protect sensitive intentions.

– Watercress

Spicy and alive. Often used in old remedies to stir up circulation. In magic, it stirs energy, quickens stale situations, and brings clarity. Associated with truth-telling and removing emotional blockages.

– Jewelweed

Grows near poison ivy and often used to soothe its sting. In magical terms, it teaches us that the cure often grows close to the wound. Jewelweed is a plant of restoration and balance.

– Elder

Sometimes found on damp edges. Sacred to the dead and the fae. You don't cut elderwood without permission. Its flowers protect. Its berries feed spirit. Its hollow branches carry whispers if you listen.

– Milkweed

Used for transformation. Hosts the monarch butterfly. Where milkweed grows, change is near. Used in spells of growth, movement, and gentle release.

– Dock
A grounding plant, often found in moist, disturbed ground. Used for luck, purification, and restoring equilibrium after trauma. Dock seeds are carried for abundance.

– Reed
A plant of sound and rhythm. Used in old flutes and charms for communication. In magic, it helps with clarity of voice and spiritual music—especially when calling to ancestors or spirits near water.

GATHERING BY THE WATER'S EDGE

If you're harvesting along a creek or riverbank, remember this: water watches. You are a guest. Harvest only what you need, and ask before cutting. Whisper your name. State your purpose. Offer a coin, a song, or a drop of honey in return.

Never harvest alone near moving water without protection. Wear iron, salt, or a plant ally like rosemary. Spirits are curious by the shore. Some just want to listen. Others want to follow.

Look for signs before you pick. If a plant is half-submerged, tangled in fishing line, or already broken—leave it. That's a warning telling you not to bring a tangled mess into your own life.

Gather during a waxing moon for growth spells, and waning moon for release or banishing. Water amplifies moon work. The closer you are to the tide's pull, the stronger the result.

RITUAL – SENDING A SPELL DOWNSTREAM

Use this spell when you need to let something go but want to mark the release with purpose.

Write your burden on a piece of biodegradable paper. This could be a name, a memory, or a question.

Tie it gently to a bundle of river-safe herbs. Try willow bark for grief, watercress for truth, or dock for balance.

Stand at the water's edge at dusk. Dusk is the best hour for endings that don't need anger.

Speak aloud: "I give you this weight. Let the water wear it smooth. Let it roll to the sea and vanish."

Release the bundle and turn away without watching it drift. The spell is in the surrender.

WEEDS THAT WATCH

Some riverside weeds don't get the love they deserve. But ask any rootworker who's done cleanings by the creek, and they'll tell you—those weeds see everything.

Smartweed, also called water pepper, is used to protect against jealousy and gossip. A plant that "bites" back.

Plantain is a healer, found where feet walk and wounds open. Use in floor washes and rootwork for spiritual first aid.

Cleavers are clingy and binding. Used in love spells and to spiritually "catch" what's drifting away from you.

Yarrow is often found near river trails. Used for protection, courage, and psychic shielding. In Appalachian tradition, it's planted by thresholds to keep away the wandering dead.

These aren't rare plants. But they're powerful because of where they grow.

WORKING WATER INTO SPELLWORK

You don't always need the plant. Sometimes the river itself is the spell.

Dip a cloth in river water and use it to cleanse a photo or object. This removes lingering energy and restores flow.

Use river pebbles on your altar to anchor a spell. Especially helpful in work related to change, forgiveness, or emotional closure.

Collect river water during a thunderstorm for added strength. This becomes storm water—ideal for justice spells or breaking stagnant patterns.

Float candles with herbs downstream for long-distance intention casting. Use this only where it's

safe and allowed. The river doesn't need our trash—
only our trust.

RIVER SPIRITS AND PLANT ALLIES

In some folk traditions, rivers are seen as mothers.
Others call them witches, saints, or sleeping dragons.
Whatever name you use, the river has memory. It
remembers what you bring to it. If you approach with
respect, it may offer gifts: a perfect feather, an
untouched flower, a stone shaped like a heart.

When working with river spirits, speak your name.
Leave offerings of natural beauty—petals, clean
coins, unwrapped fruit. Never take without giving.
Never lie near running water during heavy grief—
water listens, and it may pull too hard.

Some people keep river stones on their altars to
remind them of flow. Some keep dried river weeds in
sachets for guidance during times of emotional
confusion. And some return to the same creek year
after year, casting the same spell with new intentions.
Because magic is repetition with purpose. And rivers
are always willing to receive.

THE CONJURE DOCTOR'S GARDEN

When you step into this work as a professional magical worker, not just as a passion, the roots you use carry more than your own hopes. They carry your client's fears. Their pain. Their wishes. Their trust. You're not just making magic—you're making medicine for the spirit, and sometimes, that medicine is bitter.

A working conjure doctor doesn't just keep pretty herbs. They keep what works. Roots that hold power across different kinds of cases. Leaves that bring in luck and push out poison. Seeds that move things in courtrooms, bedrooms, job sites, and graveyards. You need a shelf that speaks the language of results.

Here's the deeper stock. The herbs you keep behind the counter. The ones you use when someone comes to your door not for advice, but for change.

FOR CASE WORK AND COURTROOM SUCCESS

– Gravel Root
Also called Joe-Pye Weed. Used to sway court decisions, smooth over legal troubles, and gain favor in bureaucratic systems. Add to court case candles or carry in a mojo bag when attending hearings.

– Devil's Shoe String
Not actually a shoe or a string—this root is used for protection from law enforcement, tricks, and

spiritual entrapment. It's often tied and worn around the ankle. Keeps clients out of jail and breaks malicious works.

– Deer's Tongue

Used for eloquence, speech magic, and winning over judges, bosses, or public figures. Excellent for those needing verbal advantage. Mix with licorice root for influence or with five finger grass for overall success.

FOR REVERSING CURSES AND CLEARING CROSSED CONDITIONS

– Agrimony

Known for turning back what was sent. If a client has been jinxed or quietly worked on, agrimony uncovers and returns it. Steep in baths or sprinkle on their threshold to break hidden workings.

– Asafoetida (Devil's Dung)

Smells awful. Works strong. Used to drive out evil spirits, negative entities, or people who show up with heavy, manipulative energy. Burned with black pepper and sulfur to clear out crossed houses. I suggest if you are going to burn this one to do it outside. Trust me.

– Sulfur

Not a plant, but crucial. Used with herbs to seal protective work or drive a target far away. In breakup jars and war water, sulfur adds fire to the working. Mix with graveyard dirt to command spirits when justified.

FOR MONEY DRAWING, BUSINESS, AND PROSPERITY CLIENTS

– Alfalfa
For keeping money in the home and warding off poverty. Store it in a jar near your cash register or altar. Combine with basil for luck in business.

– Irish Moss
Not a true moss, but used for money-drawing spells, gambling, and financial flow. Add to green candles or stuff into wallets or purses.

– Five Finger Grass (Cinquefoil)
Grants favor in all five areas of life—love, money, health, power, and luck. Especially good for clients who want "everything at once." Carry in a mojo or use in spiritual baths before job interviews or court.

FOR LOVE, SEPARATION, AND INFLUENCE

– Calamus Root
For domination, verbal control, and strong influence. Use in love work when your client needs to be heard or when they want someone to act right. Often mixed into oils or powders.

– Licorice Root
Used to compel or bend someone's will. Softens communication while reinforcing your client's intentions. Excellent in written petitions or mouth-working spells.

– Black Cohosh

For breakup work, especially where abuse or manipulation is present. Helps sever cords and remove one person's influence from another's life. Steep in vinegar or use in uncrossing lamps.

FOR ONGOING PROTECTION BETWEEN CLIENTS

– Angelica Root

Sacred to many conjure doctors and spiritual workers. Used for personal protection, strength, and ancestral covering. Keep a whole root on your altar, or grind and sprinkle it after intense work.

– Rue

An all-purpose protection herb, especially against jealousy, gossip, and the evil eye. Hang it near your front door or add to cleansing baths. Rue is sharp, ancient, and never to be used casually.

– Bayberry Root Bark

Used to secure income and keep financial blessings from slipping away. Add to spell jars, dress candles, or keep in your work apron if you handle money. "Bayberry for bucks," the old folks used to say.

PRACTICAL WISDOM FOR ROOTWORKERS

– Rotate your supplies seasonally

Herbs have lifespans. Old roots lose their edge. Refresh stock at least twice a year and always bless new material before use.

– Keep a record of every case
Write down what herbs were used, when, and for what reason. Not just for memory, but for pattern recognition. Spirit speaks through repetition.

– Don't mix baneful and blessing materials
Use different jars, different trays, even different mortar and pestles. Cleansing work and hexing work should never share tools. The energy will tangle.

– Clean your tools between clients
Pass scissors, knives, jars, and cloths through rosemary or saltwater after use. This keeps their work separate and your altar from carrying what doesn't belong.

– Feed your working herbs spiritually
Talk to them. Blow over them. Lay your hands on the jars. A conjure doctor's herbs are not just storage—they're your partners in the work.

The more cases you take, the more your herb cabinet becomes a living book. It will change with your experience. It will respond to the kind of spirits you call, the prayers you speak, and the pain you're asked to witness. A working doctor's tools don't have to be rare—but they do have to be real.

When working court case magic, one powerful trick is to get the judge's full name—first, middle, and last if possible. Write it down on a piece of brown paper torn from a grocery bag (always tear, never cut), then draw an "X" over both eyes and the mouth. This symbolic gesture is meant to "bind the eyes" so the judge can't see your faults, and "shut the mouth" so they won't speak harsh judgment. Fold the paper away from you if you're seeking leniency or dismissal—toward you if you're compelling the judge to rule in your favor.

SPELLS FROM THE GARDEN AND THE WOODS

A magical practitioner's power doesn't come from how many herbs they own. It comes from knowing how to use what they've got. You don't need a wall of jars to work strong. You need clarity. Purpose. Spirit. And a few good plants that answer when called.

The spells in this chapter are drawn from every root, flower, and leaf we've walked with so far. They're laid out plainly—no fluff, no fantasy. Each one can be worked with tools you likely already have. Add your will, your prayer, and your fire. That's where the power lives.

CLEANSING, UNCROSSING, AND PROTECTION

Hyssop Bath for Spiritual Forgiveness
Boil hyssop in water. Let cool. Strain and add to a tub of warm water. Bathe from head to toe while reciting Psalm 51. Air dry. Pour leftover water at a crossroads and walk away without looking back.

Rue Wash for the Evil Eye
Add a handful of dried rue to a bucket of mop water. Use to cleanse your home after envy, gossip, or spiritual attack. Wash toward the door, then pour out the water past your property line.

Bay Leaf Binding for Protection
Write your name on one bay leaf and the name of a

troublemaker on another. Sandwich a pinch of salt between the leaves and tie with red thread. Bury in a jar of dirt at the back of your property to stop their influence.

Red Pepper Mirror Box for Reversal
Break a small mirror into pieces. Place your enemy's name written in black ink in a box with red pepper, sulfur, and a pinch of graveyard dirt. Seal and bury in a thorn bush.

Agrimony Sachet for Reversal and Return
Fill a black cloth pouch with agrimony, mustard seed, and salt. Carry on you when walking through a place where someone has worked against you. It sends harm back without returning it in kind.

Mullein Smoke for Spirit Warding
Burn mullein leaves over charcoal to keep malicious spirits out of your house after heavy work. Walk the smoke through corners and around thresholds.

LOVE, ATTRACTION, AND RELATIONSHIP WORK

Pink Rose Bath to Mend a Heart
Steep dried pink rose petals in hot water. Strain and pour into a bath with honey and a splash of Florida water. Bathe while speaking aloud what you're ready to release and what you wish to receive.

Basil Love Jar for Sweetening
Write your target's name on parchment. Add basil, sugar, and a drop of rose oil. Fold toward you and

place in a small jar with honey. Burn a pink candle on top every Friday until your desire is fulfilled.

Honeysuckle Tie Binding
For someone straying emotionally. Write your name and theirs on a strip of white cloth. Rub with honeysuckle oil. Tie in a knot and bury under your bedroom window to draw the heart home.

Calamus and Licorice Influence Bottle
Combine calamus root, licorice root, your written command, and personal concern into a bottle. Seal with red wax. Shake daily to keep your target under your influence.

Passionflower Peace Candle for Couples
Dress a white candle with passionflower tea and lavender oil. Light on Fridays with a prayer for understanding. Best done before important conversations.

MONEY, LUCK, AND SUCCESS

Five Finger Grass Mojo for Favor
Fill a red flannel bag with five finger grass, alfalfa, basil, and a silver dime. Dress with cinnamon oil. Feed weekly with whiskey and carry for luck in job interviews or business.

Irish Moss Gambling Powder
Grind Irish moss and alfalfa with a pinch of cinnamon. Sprinkle into shoes or your wallet before visiting the casino or playing numbers.

Bayberry Root Bark Jar for Steady Income

Add bayberry root bark, salt, and coins to a green jar. Seal and place near the front door. Shake daily to keep money flowing and bills paid.

Chamomile Court Case Candle

Dress a white or yellow candle with chamomile oil. Carve the case number or names into the wax. Burn on the day of your court appearance with Psalm 35 or 37.

Cinnamon Quick Draw Charm

Wrap cinnamon sticks in gold fabric with sugar and a lodestone. Carry when you need fast money or to close a deal quickly.

CURSING, BREAKUP, AND BANEFUL WORK

Black Cohosh Separation Vinegar

Soak black cohosh and red pepper in vinegar for seven days. Write the couple's names, cut apart, and add to the jar. Shake daily. Bury at a three-way crossroads.

Morning Glory Binding Cord

Write a behavior or influence you want to stop on paper. Wrap it in morning glory vine and tie tight. Hide it in a dark place until the binding takes hold.

Poppy Seed Confusion Spell

Add poppy seeds to a black candle and burn it upside-down on a photo of your target. Speak aloud your command to mislead, distract, or confuse.

Mustard Seed War Jar

Combine black mustard seeds, cayenne, sulfur, and nail clippings in a sealed jar. Shake to sow chaos or unrest. Dispose far from home.

Asafoetida Boundary Burn

Write your enemy's name and cross it out. Sprinkle with asafoetida. Burn over charcoal and bury the ashes away from your home.

DREAMWORK, VISION, AND SPIRIT TRAVEL

Mugwort Dream Pillow

Sew mugwort, lavender, and violet into a pouch. Sleep with it near your head to invite spirit dreams. Write what you see when you wake.

Blue Lotus Wine Spell for Trance

Soak blue lotus in red wine for three nights. Sip slowly while sitting before a black candle and asking for ancestral contact.

Passionflower Sleep Jar

Layer passionflower, hops, and chamomile into a jar. Seal with blue wax. Keep near your bed to ease restless sleep and open dream sight.

ANCESTOR AND SPIRIT WORK

Marigold Altar Circle

Place marigolds in a ring around your ancestor candle. Speak their names. Offer food, water, or tobacco. Repeat on holy days or family anniversaries.

Rose and Frankincense Smoke for Ancestors
Burn dried rose petals with frankincense to call peaceful spirits. Use to anoint photos or personal items tied to loved ones who've passed.

Grave Flower Petition
Write a letter to your ancestor. Wrap in white rose petals and bury near a tree or stone. Ask for guidance in dreams.

HEALING, PEACE, AND SPIRITUAL FORTIFICATION

Angelica Protection Bowl
Place angelica root in a bowl with salt, rosemary, and a piece of iron. Keep near your front door to shield from harm and spiritual heaviness.

Lavender Floor Wash for Emotional Calm
Steep lavender, chamomile, and basil in boiling water. Let cool. Strain and wash the home from back to front. Burn white candles afterward to reset energy.

Elderflower Peace Tea (External Use Only)
Make a light tea with dried elderflower and mugwort. Use in baths or room sprays to bring softness and spiritual comfort during grief or transition.

These spells aren't suggestions. They're tools.
Use them with respect and conviction when it's time to move the spirit world—and stir the physical one into motion.

CONCLUSION

Botanical magic is a path of listening. It begins in the soil, moves through the hands, and settles in the heart. It teaches you that every plant has a voice, every flower has a history, and every root remembers where it came from.

The plants in this book have walked through cemeteries and churchyards. They've been tucked into hymnals, burned at crossroads, crushed beneath the boots of field workers, and offered in silence at hospital bedsides. They carry memory and power.

Whether you're gathering hyssop for cleansing, licorice root for persuasion, or marigolds to honor the dead, the work only deepens when you approach it with humility. That's what separates spellcasting from spiritual service.

As your knowledge grows, your relationship with the plants will change. Some will fall away. Others will come forward. That's the nature of living magic. It grows. It roots. It remembers.

And now, so do you.

Papa Gee

CAUTION & WARNING – POISONOUS PLANTS

Not every plant is meant to be touched. Some bite back. Some fool the senses. And some carry spirits that don't care whether you meant well—they care whether you came with wisdom.

Working with baneful plants demands clarity, respect, and caution. This is not just about spiritual danger. Some herbs can harm your body if used incorrectly. Others can confuse your mind or open doors you're not ready to walk through. Magic, like medicine, is not a game. The spirits of these plants are old, sharp, and watchful. If you misuse them, they will teach you— and it won't be gentle.

This list includes every plant in the book known to be **toxic**, **psychoactive**, or **dangerous if ingested, inhaled, or improperly handled**. Some should never be burned. Others should never be taken internally. Most of them should be used only symbolically or under the guidance of an experienced practitioner. In fact, I would prefer that you leave these plants alone all together to be on the safe side. Remember that an ounce of prevention is worth a pound of cure. I included these plants for historical purposes. There's nothing "glamorous" or extra "witchy" about using poisonous plants. Use a safer replacement and leave the harmful plants alone.

PLANTS THAT ARE POISONOUS OR REQUIRE EXTRA CAUTION

– **Belladonna (Deadly Nightshade)**

 – **Mandrake Root** (real species, not symbolic stand-ins)

 – **Datura (Jimsonweed, Moonflower)**

 – **Henbane**

 – **Aconite (Wolfsbane, Monkshood)**

 – **Foxglove**

 – **Hemlock** (Poison Hemlock, not conifer)

 – **Rue** – can cause skin irritation and is toxic in large amounts

 – **Bloodroot** – the sap can be caustic and should not be taken internally

 – **Lily (especially Easter Lily)** – toxic to pets and in high doses

 – **Hyacinth** – bulbs are toxic if ingested

 – **Poppy (especially Oriental and Opium varieties)** – contains alkaloids; do not ingest

 – **Yew** – highly poisonous if consumed

 – **Elder (raw berries, bark, leaves)** – toxic unless properly prepared

 – **Laburnum** – ornamental tree, extremely toxic

 – **Bryony** – highly toxic root used in European folklore

 – **Fern Flower (mythic)** – while not real, be cautious of certain ferns which can be toxic to pets

 – **Lotus of Forgetfulness (mythic)** – associated with altered states; do not attempt to mimic with lookalike plants

 – **Alraun (Mandrake Spirit Root)** – if using substitutes like mayapple, note that it is also toxic

Important Warnings

- Never ingest any herb unless you are 100% certain of its identity, safety, and dosage and even then, triple check your sources.

- Do not burn toxic herbs indoors or in closed spaces.

- Keep all baneful herbs away from children, pets, and those with respiratory conditions.

- Use gloves and avoid touching your face or eyes after handling these plants.

- Symbolic use—such as drawing the plant, naming it in ritual, or using prepared correspondences—is often safer and just as effective.

Magic has rules. Not laws written on paper, but laws written in consequence. The plants on this list aren't here to be feared—but they must be respected. They teach through edge, not ease. And if you can't meet them with a steady hand and a clean heart, leave them be.

SPELL INDEX

Animal and Spirit Connection

– *Ritual for Animal–Plant Spirit Alignment* – Connects a specific herb or root to a chosen animal spirit for guidance or totemic work – Chapter 18

– *Reading Plant Signatures for Animal Messages* – Uses leaf shape, scent, or behavior of a plant to reveal messages tied to familiar spirits or animal omens – Chapter 18

Ancestor Work & Remembrance

– *Grave Flower Offering for a Departed Loved One* – Lays sacred blooms at a grave to honor and connect with ancestors – Chapter 14

– *Ritual to Speak Their Name with a Bloom* – Uses a flower and candle to call on the name and spirit of a specific ancestor – Chapter 14

– *Using Dried Funeral Flowers in Spirit Magic* – Employs petals from funerals for charm bags, oils, or jars that maintain spiritual connection – Chapter 14

– *Marigold Altar Circle for Ancestor Calling* – Places marigolds around an altar or photo to guide and invite benevolent spirit visitation – Chapter 21

– *Rose and Frankincense Smoke for Ancestors* – Burned as a devotional offering to draw peace, memory, and gratitude – Chapter 21

– *Grave Flower Petition for Dream Messages* – Writes a note to the dead wrapped in flowers and buried to call for dream contact – Chapter 21

Astrological Timing

– *Working with Planetary Herb Power* – Aligns plant choices with planetary rulerships for better spell outcomes – Chapter 12

– *Aligning Spell Timing to Planet Days* – Matches each day of the week with herbs, planets, and magical goals – Chapter 12

Banishing & Protection

– *Herb Bundle for Home and Spirit Protection* – Bundled protective herbs are hung near doors or burned to seal and guard space – Chapter 3

– *Baneful Plant Awareness for Hex and Curse Work* – Explains how dangerous herbs teach caution, shadow work, and defense – Chapter 8

– Saturn-Aligned Binding or Endings Work – Uses heavy Saturn herbs to close roads, bind actions, or sever ties – Chapter 12

– Bay Leaf Binding to Stop Harm – Ties names in bay leaves with salt to block gossip, spiritual attack, or unwanted influence – Chapter 21

– Red Pepper Mirror Box for Reversal – Reflects enemy intent back on them using hot pepper and mirror shards – Chapter 21

– Agrimony Sachet to Send a Curse Back – A quiet way to reverse a jinx without confrontation – Chapter 21

– Mullein Smoke to Ward Off Spirits – Burned to protect from hauntings or baneful presences – Chapter 21

– Angelica Protection Bowl at the Door – A bowl of roots, salt, and iron to stop harmful energy from entering – Chapter 21

Blessing & Cleansing

– Sacred Herb Blessing Bundle – Combines cedar, rosemary, or basil for smoke blessing and house clearing – Chapter 3

– Ritual for Consecrating a Tree or Plant Ally – Establishes a spiritual bond with a living plant guardian – Chapter 7

– Flower Bath for Spiritual Peace – A rose- and lavender-based bath for emotional healing and aura softening – Chapter 13

– Hyssop Bath for Spiritual Forgiveness – Biblical cleansing to prepare for magic after wrongdoing or guilt – Chapter 21

– Rue Wash for the Evil Eye – Traditional mop water recipe to break envy, hexes, and jinxes in the home – Chapter 21

– Lavender Floor Wash for Emotional Calm – A soothing herbal wash to shift tension, sadness, or spiritual static – Chapter 21

Cursing, Breakup, and Baneful Work

– Mandrake (or Substitute) Root Spirit Spell – Awakens a carved or whole root for deep spiritual working or dark protection – Chapter 8

– Black Cohosh Separation Vinegar – Breaks up lovers or toxic bonds with vinegar and breaking roots – Chapter 21

– Morning Glory Binding Cord – Ties a behavior or person symbolically using binding vine – Chapter 21

– Poppy Seed Confusion Spell – Causes misdirection and forgetfulness when a target needs distraction – Chapter 21

– Mustard Seed War Jar – Sows spiritual unrest using black mustard, sulfur, and personal concern – Chapter 21

– Asafoetida Boundary Burn – Drives away unwanted people or

lingering energies with powerful smoke – Chapter 21

Dreamwork & Psychic Vision

– *Root and Crown Centering Ritual* – Grounds the body and opens spiritual sight using plant focus – Chapter 1
– *Mugwort Dream Pillow or Incense Use* – Encourages lucid dreaming, prophecy, and spirit contact during sleep – Chapters 6, 9, 12, 21
– *Blue Lotus Wine for Trance Work* – Prepared to induce a visionary or spiritual state for ritual – Chapter 21
– *Passionflower Sleep Jar* – Soothes nightmares and enhances safe astral wandering – Chapter 21

Grief & Release

– *Flower Offering for Grief Expression* – A simple floral devotion to speak what can't be said – Chapter 14
– *Planting a Bloom in Memory* – Plants grown in mourning to hold memory and mark loss – Chapter 14
– *Elderflower Peace Tea for Grieving (External Use)* – A bath or spray for calming heartache and easing transition – Chapter 21

Initiation & Shadow Work

– *Working with Mythic Plants for Inner Change* – Uses symbolic herbs (like datura or fern) in rites of passage – Chapter 15
– *Symbolic Use of Fern Flower for Soul Growth* – Connects to unseen potential and rare insight – Chapter 6
– *Listening Tree Spirit Ritual* – A method of silent communion with a sacred tree – Chapter 7

Love & Attraction

– *Using Venus-Aligned Herbs in Love Spells* – Explains how to choose herbs by planetary rulership – Chapter 12
– *Flower Charm for Quiet Devotion* – Uses a violet or rose to send a silent but powerful romantic signal – Chapter 13
– *Rose Petal Petition Ritual* – Wraps a name in love-drenched petals for drawing or healing – Chapter 13
– *Pink Rose Bath for Heart Mending* – Comforts grief after a breakup or emotional rupture – Chapter 21
– *Basil Love Jar for Sweetening* – A honey jar to soften and call someone

closer – Chapter 21
 – *Honeysuckle Tie Binding for Emotional Loyalty* – Used to keep hearts from straying – Chapter 21
 – *Calamus and Licorice Influence Bottle* – Strengthens your voice in a relationship or persuasive working – Chapter 21
 – *Passionflower Candle for Calm in Love* – A gentle peace-working between quarreling partners – Chapter 21

Money, Luck & Success

 – *Five Finger Grass Mojo Bag* – Draws luck in money, court, love, health, and favor – Chapter 21
 – *Irish Moss Gambling Powder* – Boosts winning streaks and financial pull – Chapter 21
 – *Bayberry Root Bark Jar for Steady Income* – Seals long-term money flow and financial stability – Chapter 21
 – *Chamomile Candle for Court Favor* – A simple but strong working for judges, trials, and decisions – Chapter 21
 – *Cinnamon Quick Draw Charm* – Used when fast money or immediate results are needed – Chapter 21

Plant Communication & Magical Listening

 – *Reading the Signature of a Plant* – Interpreting plant shapes and behaviors for spiritual meaning – Chapter 11
 – *Spirit Interview with a Single Herb* – A guided ritual to meet the indwelling energy of a plant – Chapter 11
 – *Flower Language Offering on an Altar* – An arrangement chosen with intentional symbolism for spirit communication – Chapter 13
 – *Petition to the Guardian Tree* – Ritual to ask protection or permission from a sacred tree – Chapter 2

Wishes, Offerings & Fae Work

 – *Fairy Offering Dish for Peaceful Relations* – A respectful gesture to the Good Folk, placed near garden or threshold – Chapter 6
 – *Drawing on Plant–Animal Energy for Spirit Work* – Uses paired natural forces to enhance magical alignment – Chapter 18

MAGICAL MATERIALS INDEX

Agrimony

– **Properties:** Reversal, uncrossing, spiritual armor
– **Uses:** Reverses jinxes, breaks secret curses, protects from hidden enemies
– **Chapters:** 8, 20, 21

Alfalfa

– **Properties:** Prosperity, protection from poverty
– **Uses:** Keeps money in the home, protects against financial hardship
– **Chapters:** 20, 21

Angelica Root

– **Properties:** Protection, spiritual strength, ancestor connection
– **Uses:** Wards off harm, empowers mojo bags, blesses sacred space
– **Chapters:** 20, 21

Asafoetida

– **Properties:** Banishment, exorcism, boundary enforcement
– **Uses:** Drives away spirits, breaks curses, protects from spiritual intrusion
– **Chapters:** 8, 20, 21

Basil

– **Properties:** Love, luck, protection
– **Uses:** Attracts love or money, sweetens energy, wards off jealousy
– **Chapters:** 3, 13, 20, 21

Bay Leaf

– **Properties:** Protection, success, divination
– **Uses:** Used in wish magic, name paper spells, and dreamwork
– **Chapters:** 3, 7, 20, 21

Bayberry Root Bark

– **Properties:** Money drawing, stability
– **Uses:** Keeps income flowing, protects financial blessings
– **Chapters:** 20, 21

Belladonna

– **Properties:** Spirit sight, trance, shadow work
– **Uses:** Used carefully in dark or necromantic rituals
– **Chapters:** 8, 10

Black Cohosh

– **Properties:** Separation, cutting ties
– **Uses:** Breaks unhealthy bonds, used in breakup and domination work
– **Chapters:** 20, 21

Blue Lotus

– **Properties:** Trance, vision, spiritual ecstasy
– **Uses:** Induces altered states and dreamwork when steeped or smoked
– **Chapters:** 9, 21

Calamus Root

– **Properties:** Control, command, influence
– **Uses:** Used in court case work, verbal domination, and leadership rituals
– **Chapters:** 8, 20, 21

Carnation

– **Properties:** Grief, remembrance, strength
– **Uses:** Added to funeral flowers and spirit offerings
– **Chapters:** 14

Cedar

– **Properties:** Cleansing, peace, protection

– **Uses:** Burned in bundles, added to floor washes or placed at entryways
– **Chapters:** 3, 14

Chamomile

– **Properties:** Peace, luck, justice
– **Uses:** Used in calming rituals, court work, and emotional healing
– **Chapters:** 3, 13, 20, 21

Cinnamon

– **Properties:** Speed, attraction, success
– **Uses:** Added to fast-acting spells, love work, and prosperity jars
– **Chapters:** 20, 21

Dandelion

– **Properties:** Divination, spirit contact, wishes
– **Uses:** Used in communication with the dead or spirit-led decisions
– **Chapters:** 16

Deer's Tongue

– **Properties:** Eloquence, persuasion, speech
– **Uses:** Improves communication, court cases, and public favor
– **Chapters:** 20

Devil's Shoe String

– **Properties:** Protection, legal defense
– **Uses:** Prevents arrest, breaks tricks, worn for spiritual protection
– **Chapters:** 20

Elder / Elderflower

– **Properties:** Spirit contact, protection, dreamwork
– **Uses:** Used in honoring the dead, fairy rites, and emotional healing
– **Chapters:** 6, 14, 21

Fern

– **Properties:** Mystery, spirit initiation, hidden knowledge
– **Uses:** Used for self-growth and magical awakening
– **Chapters:** 6, 15

Five Finger Grass (Cinquefoil)

– **Properties:** Luck, success in five areas: love, money, health, power, and luck
– **Uses:** Carried in mojos or added to spell jars
– **Chapters:** 20, 21

Foxglove

– **Properties:** Fairy communication, warning, psychic protection
– **Uses:** Symbol of spirit activity and psychic sensitivity
– **Chapters:** 6, 10

Frankincense

– **Properties:** Purification, spirit elevation, prayer
– **Uses:** Burned in rituals for blessing, ancestor contact, or offerings
– **Chapters:** 3, 14

Gravel Root (Joe-Pye Weed)

– **Properties:** Legal success, favor, clarity
– **Uses:** Used in court case mojos or added to legal candles
– **Chapters:** 20

Hawthorn

– **Properties:** Fairy protection, love boundaries
– **Uses:** Grown to honor fairies or to shield love spells from harm
– **Chapters:** 6

Hemlock

– **Properties:** Silence, separation, spiritual cutting
– **Uses:** Symbolic severing of ties, not used physically
– **Chapters:** 8

Honeysuckle

– **Properties:** Attraction, binding, devotion
– **Uses:** Draws in loyalty and emotional closeness
– **Chapters:** 20, 21

Hops

– **Properties:** Sleep, surrender, grief support
– **Uses:** Added to dream pillows and soothing teas
– **Chapters:** 9

Hyssop

– **Properties:** Cleansing, repentance, spiritual purity
– **Uses:** Used in spiritual baths and pre-spell preparation
– **Chapters:** 3, 12, 20, 21

Irish Moss

– **Properties:** Gambling luck, business prosperity
– **Uses:** Carried for luck in games of chance or placed in registers
– **Chapters:** 20, 21

Lavender

– **Properties:** Peace, devotion, restful sleep
– **Uses:** Used in dreamwork, love spells, or floor washes
– **Chapters:** 3, 9, 13, 21

Licorice Root

– **Properties:** Domination, persuasion
– **Uses:** Used to sweeten or control a person or situation
– **Chapters:** 20, 21

Mandrake (and Substitutes)

– **Properties:** Spirit power, fertility, dream contact
– **Uses:** Used in deep spiritual work or to awaken spell jars
– **Chapters:** 8, 15

Marigold

– **Properties:** Ancestor work, protection, joy
 – **Uses:** Used during Day of the Dead, altars, or dream visitations
 – **Chapters:** 4, 14, 21

Morning Glory

– **Properties:** Binding, entanglement
 – **Uses:** Symbolically knots behavior or emotional patterns
 – **Chapters:** 8, 21

Mugwort

– **Properties:** Psychic sight, dreams, prophecy
 – **Uses:** Burned or steeped for dream pillows, divination, or ritual vision
 – **Chapters:** 6, 9, 12, 20, 21

Mullein

– **Properties:** Spirit calling, protection, grave work
 – **Uses:** Burned in ritual or added to ancestor jars
 – **Chapters:** 8, 20, 21

Mustard Seed (Black)

– **Properties:** Confusion, disruption
 – **Uses:** Used to scatter attention or sow unrest
 – **Chapters:** 8, 21

Poppy Seed

– **Properties:** Confusion, sleep, distraction
 – **Uses:** Used to cause someone to misstep, forget, or lose clarity
 – **Chapters:** 8, 21

Passionflower

– **Properties:** Calm, peace in love, sleep
 – **Uses:** Used in relationship healing and dream spells
 – **Chapters:** 9, 13, 21

Red Pepper / Cayenne

– **Properties:** Banishing, domination, aggression
  – **Uses:** Used in hot foot, breakup, or commanding spells
  – **Chapters:** 3, 8, 20, 21

Rose (Red, White, Pink)

– **Properties:** Love, grief, remembrance
  – **Uses:** Used in spiritual baths, ancestor altars, or dreamwork
  – **Chapters:** 4, 13, 14, 21

Rosemary

– **Properties:** Memory, purification, mental clarity
  – **Uses:** Burned or steeped for cleansing and strengthening
  – **Chapters:** 3, 20

Rue

– **Properties:** Protection, uncrossing, reversal
  – **Uses:** Used in baths and home cleansings, strong against envy
  – **Chapters:** 3, 12, 20, 21

St. John's Wort

– **Properties:** Protection, strength, midsummer power
  – **Uses:** Burned or carried to repel dark spirits and depression
  – **Chapters:** 12

Sulfur (not a plant, but included)

– **Properties:** Hexing, banishment, spiritual fire
  – **Uses:** Combined with herbs in war jars and reversal work
  – **Chapters:** 8, 20

BIBLIOGRAPHY

Andrews, Jean. *The Texas Herbal: A Guide to Native and Adapted Plants*. University of Texas Press. 2006.

Folkard, Richard. *Plant Lore, Legends, and Lyrics*. Sampson Low, Marston, Searle, and Rivington. 1884.

Beck, Horace. *Folklore and the Sea*. Wesleyan University Press. 1973.

Crellin, John K. and Jane Philpott. *A Reference Guide to Medicinal Plants: Herbal Medicine Past and Present*. Duke University Press. 1990.

Fett, Sharla M. *Working Cures: Healing, Health, and Power on Southern Slave Plantations*. University of North Carolina Press. 2002.

Gifford, Paul. *African American Magic and Hoodoo: A Historical Reader*. Indiana University Press. 2014.

Grieve, Maud. *A Modern Herbal: The Medicinal, Culinary, Cosmetic and Economic Properties, Cultivation and Folklore of Herbs, Grasses, Fungi, Shrubs and Trees*. Dover Publications. 1971.

Hatfield, Gabrielle. *Encyclopedia of Folk Medicine: Old World and New World Traditions*. ABC-CLIO. 2003.

Hecht, Jennifer Michael. *The End of the Soul: Scientific Modernity, Atheism, and Anthropology in France*. Columbia University Press. 2003.

Jones, LuAnn. *Mama Learned Us to Work: Farm Women in the New South*. University of North Carolina Press. 2002.

McNeill, F. Marian. *The Silver Bough: A Four Volume Study of Scottish Folklore and Folk Belief*. Canongate Books. 1992.

Moerman, Daniel E. *Native American Ethnobotany*. Timber Press. 1998.

Puckett, Newbell Niles. *Folk Beliefs of the Southern Negro*. University of North Carolina Press. 1926.

Storl, Wolf D. *The Herbal Lore of Wise Women and Wortcunners: The Healing Power of Medicinal Plants*. North Atlantic Books. 2012.

Thompson, Robert Farris. *Flash of the Spirit: African and Afro-American Art and Philosophy*. Vintage Books. 1984.

Yronwode, Catherine. *Hoodoo Herb and Root Magic: A Materia Magica of African-American Conjure*. Lucky Mojo Curio Co. 2002.